NOAM CHOMSKY

MODERN MASTERS

Already published

MODERN MASTERS

EDITED BY frank kermode

noam chomsky

john lyons

NEW YORK | THE VIKING PRESS

Published in 1970 in a hardbound
and a paperback edition
by The Viking Press, Inc.
625 Madison Avenue, New York, N.Y. 10022

SBN 670–51473–x (hardbound)
670–01911–9 (paperback)

Library of Congress catalog card number: 73–104148

Printed in U.S.A.

Fifth printing August 1972

PREFACE

I should like to record here my gratitude to Noam Chomsky for reading and commenting upon the manuscript of this book. The fact that it has been read in advance by Chomsky (and corrected in a number of places) encourages me in the belief that it gives a reasonably fair and reliable account of his views on linguistics and the philosophy of language. There are of course a number of points, especially in the final chapter, where Chomsky is not in entire agreement with what I have to say. But these points of disagreement will be obvious enough either from the text itself or from the footnotes that I have added.

My main purpose in writing the book has been to provide the reader with enough of the historical and technical background for him to go on afterward to Chomsky's own works. I am aware that certain sections of my book are fairly demanding. But I do not believe that it is possible to understand even Chomsky's less technical works or to appreciate the impact his ideas are having in a number of different disciplines without going into some of the details of the formal system for the description of language that he has constructed.

J. C. Marshall and P. H. Matthews have also been kind enough to read the book for me in manuscript; and I have made many changes in the final version as a result of their comments. I am deeply indebted to them for their assistance. Needless to say, I am myself solely responsible for any errors or imperfections that still remain in the text.

J.L.

CONTENTS

BIOGRAPHICAL NOTE

Avram Noam Chomsky was born in Philadelphia, Pennsylvania, on December 7, 1928. He received his early education at the Oak Lane Country Day School and the Central High School, Philadelphia, and then went on to the University of Pennsylvania, where he studied linguistics, mathematics, and philosophy. It was at the University of Pennsylvania that he took his Ph.D., although most of the research that led to this degree was carried out as a Junior Fellow of the Society of Fellows at Harvard University between 1951 and 1955. Since 1955 he has taught at the Massachusetts Institute of Technology, where he now holds the Ferrari P. Ward Chair of Modern Languages and Linguistics. He is married, with two daughters and a son.

Chomsky's work has been widely acclaimed in academic circles. He has been awarded an honorary doctorate by the University of Chicago and by the University of London; and he has been invited to lecture in many different countries. In 1967 he delivered the Beckman Lectures at the University of California at Berkeley; and in 1969 he delivered the John Locke Lectures at the University of Oxford, and the Shearman Memorial Lectures at the University of London.

Chomsky first made his reputation in linguistics. He had learned something of the principles of historical linguistics from his father, who was a Hebrew scholar of considerable repute. (Chomsky himself did some of his earliest linguistic research, for the degree of M.A., on modern spoken Hebrew.) But the work for which he is now famous, the construction of a system of generative grammar, developed out of his interest in modern logic and the foundations of mathematics, and was only subsequently applied to the description of natural languages. Of considerable importance in Chomsky's intellectual development was the influence of Zellig Harris, Professor of Linguistics at the University of Pennsylvania; and Chomsky himself has explained that it was really his sympathy with Harris's political views that led him to work as an undergraduate in linguistics. There is a sense, therefore, in which politics brought him into linguistics.

Chomsky has been interested in politics since childhood. His views were formed in what he refers to as "the radical Jewish community in New York" and have always tended toward socialism or anarchism. Since 1965 he has become one of the leading critics of American foreign policy; and his recently published book of essays on this topic, *American Power and the New Mandarins* (dedicated "to the brave young men who refuse to serve in a criminal war"), is widely recognized as one of the most powerful indictments of American involvement in Vietnam that has yet appeared.

NOAM CHOMSKY

Introduction

●

1

Chomsky's position not only is unique within linguistics at the present time, but is probably unprecedented in the whole history of the subject. His first book, published in 1957, short and relatively nontechnical though it was, revolutionized the scientific study of language; and now, at the age of forty-two, he speaks with unrivaled authority on all aspects of grammatical theory. This is not to say, of course, that all linguists, or even the majority of them, have accepted the theory of transformational grammar that Chomsky put forward some thirteen years ago in *Syntactic Structures*. They have not. There are at least as many recognizably different "schools" of linguistics throughout the world as there were before the "Chomskyan revolution." But the "transformationalist," or "Chomskyan," school is not just one among many. Right or wrong,

Chomsky's theory of grammar is undoubtedly the most dynamic and influential; and no linguist who wishes to keep abreast of current developments in his subject can afford to ignore Chomsky's theoretical pronouncements. Every other "school" of linguistics at the present time tends to define its position in relation to Chomsky's views on particular issues.

However, it is not so much Chomsky's status and reputation among linguists that has made him a "master of modern thought." After all, theoretical linguistics is a rather esoteric subject, which few people had even heard of and still fewer knew anything about until very recently. If it is now more widely recognized as a branch of science that is worth while pursuing, not only for its own sake, but also for the contributions it can make to other disciplines, this is very largely due to Chomsky. More than a thousand university students and teachers are said to have attended his lectures on the philosophy of language and mind at Oxford University in the spring of 1969. Few of these could have had any previous contact with linguistics, but all of them presumably were convinced, or prepared to be convinced, that it was worth making the intellectual effort required to follow Chomsky's at times quite technical argument; and the lectures were widely reported in the national press.

Readers who are not already familiar with Chomsky's work may well be wondering at this point what possible connection there might be between a field of study as specialized as transformational grammar and such better known and obviously important disciplines as psychology and philosophy. This is a question we shall be discussing in some detail in the later chapters of this book. But it may be worth while attempting a more general answer here.

It has often been suggested that man is most clearly distinguished from other animal species, not by the faculty of thought or intelligence, as the standard zoological label "Homo sapiens" might indicate, but by his capacity for language. Indeed, philosophers and psychologists have long debated whether thought in the proper sense of the term is conceivable except as "embodied" in speech or writing. Whether or not this is so, it is obvious that language is of vital importance in every aspect of human activity and that, without language, all but the most rudimentary kind of communication would be impossible. Granted that language is essential to human life as we know it, it is only natural to ask what contribution the study of language can make to our understanding of human nature.

But what is language? This is a question that few people even think of asking. In one sense, of course, we all know what we mean by "language"; and our use of the word in everyday conversation depends upon the fact that we all interpret it, as we interpret the other words we use, in the same or in a very similar way. There is, however, a difference between this kind of unreflecting and practical knowledge of what language is and the deeper or more systematic understanding that we should want to call "scientific." As we shall see in the following chapters, it is the aim of theoretical linguistics to give a scientific answer to the question "What is language?" and, in doing so, to provide evidence that philosophers and psychologists can draw upon in their discussion of the relationship that holds between language and thought.

Chomsky's system of transformational grammar was developed, as we shall see, in order to give a mathematically precise description of some of the most striking features of language. Of particular importance in this connection is the ability that children have to derive the structural regularities of their native language—its grammatical rules—from the utterances of their parents and others around them, and then to make use of the same regularities in the construction of utterances they have never heard before. Chomsky has argued, in his most recent publications, that the general principles which determine the form of grammatical rules in particular languages, such as English, Turkish, or Chinese, are to some considerable degree common to all human languages. Furthermore, he has claimed that the principles underlying the structure of language are so specific and so highly articulated that they must be regarded as being biologically determined; that is to say, as constituting part of what we call "human nature" and as being genetically transmitted from parents to their children. If this is so, and if it is also the case, as Chomsky maintains, that transformational grammar is the best theory so far developed for the systematic description and explanation of the structure of human language, it is clear that an understanding of transformational grammar is essential for any philosopher, psychologist, or biologist who wishes to take account of man's capacity for language.

The significance of Chomsky's work for disciplines

other than linguistics derives primarily, then, from the acknowledged importance of language in all areas of human activity and from the peculiarly intimate relationship that is said to hold between the structure of language and the innate properties or operations of the mind. But language is not the only kind of complex "behavior" that human beings engage in; and there is at least a possibility that other forms of typically human activity (including, perhaps, certain aspects of what we call "artistic creation") will also prove amenable to description within the framework of specially constructed mathematical systems analogous to, or even based upon, transformational grammar. There are many scholars working now in the social sciences and the humanities who believe that this is so. For them, Chomsky's formalization of grammatical theory serves as a model and a standard.

From what has been said in the last few paragraphs it will be clear that Chomsky's influence is now being felt in many different disciplines. So far, however, it is the study of language that has been most profoundly affected by the "Chomskyan revolution"; and it is from current research on the grammatical structure of English and other languages that Chomsky draws most of his more general philosophical and psychological views. It is for this reason that we shall give so much attention in the present volume to the linguistic background of Chomsky's thought.

Chomsky's current fame and popularity are not due solely, or even mainly, to his work in linguistics and the effect that this is having on other disciplines. In the last few years he has become known as one of the most outspoken and most articulate critics of American politics in Vietnam—a "hero of the New Left"—who has risked imprisonment by refusing to pay half his taxes and has given support and encouragement to young men refusing to undertake military service in Vietnam. It is undoubtedly for his political writings and his political activity that Chomsky is now most famous, especially in the United States. Relatively few people may have read the lengthy and scholarly essays he contributed to *Liberation, Ramparts,* and *The New York Review of Books* (now collected together with other material and republished as *American Power and the New Mandarins*); but the general theme of these essays will be familiar to many—his condemnation of American "imperialism" and of those academic advisers to the American government who, posing as "experts" in a field where there is no such thing as scientific expertise and where considerations of common morality should have prevailed, have been guilty of deceiving the public about the character of the war in Vietnam, American involvement in Cuba, and other issues.

Although this book is mainly about Chomsky's views on language, it should perhaps be emphasized here that his theory of language and his political philosophy are by no means unconnected, as they might appear to be at first sight. As we shall see in the chapters that follow, Chomsky has long been an opponent of at least the more extreme form of behaviorist psychology, "radical behaviorism," according to which all human knowledge and belief, and all the "patterns" of thought and action characteristic of man, can be explained as "habits" built up by a process of "conditioning," lengthier and more complex no doubt in its details, but not qualitatively different from the process by which rats in a psychological laboratory "learn" to obtain food by pressing a bar in the cage in which they are housed. Chomsky's attack on radical behaviorism was first made in a long and well-documented review of B. F. Skinner's *Verbal Behavior* in 1959, in which Chomsky claimed that the behaviorists' impressive panoply of scientific terminology and statistics was no more than camouflage, covering up their inability to account for the fact that language simply is not a set of "habits" and is radically different from animal communication. It is the same charge that Chomsky now makes in his political writings against the sociologists, psychologists, and other social scientists whose "expert" advice is sought by governments: that they "desperately attempt . . . to imitate the surface features of sciences that really have significant intellectual content," neglecting in this attempt all the fundamental problems with which they should be concerned and taking refuge in pragmatic and methodological trivialities. It is Chomsky's conviction that human beings are different from animals or machines and that this difference should be respected both in science and in government; and it is this conviction that underlies and unifies his politics, his linguistics, and his philosophy.

Chomsky's message is familiar enough, and it will find an immediate response in all those who subscribe to a belief in the brotherhood of man and the dignity of human life. Only too often, however, the defense of these traditional values is left to scholars who by academic training are unfitted for the kind of argument that appeals to hardheaded "pragmatists." Chomsky cannot be written off quite so easily as a "woolly-minded liberal." He is as well read in the philosophy of science as his opponents are, and he can manipulate the conceptual and mathematical apparatus of the social sciences with equal ease. His arguments may be accepted or rejected: they cannot be ignored. And anyone who wishes to follow and evaluate these arguments must be prepared to meet Chomsky on his home ground: linguistics, or the scientific investigation of language. For Chomsky believes, as I said earlier, that the structure of language is determined by the structure of the human mind and that the universality of certain properties characteristic of language is evidence that at least this part of human nature is common to all members of the species, regardless of their race or class and their undoubted differences in intellect, personality, and physical attributes. This belief is quite traditional (and Chomsky himself, we shall see, explicitly relates his views to those of the rationalist philosophers of the seventeenth and eighteenth centuries). What is new is the way in which Chomsky argues his case and the kind of evidence that he adduces in support of it.

It is appropriate, and symbolic of his position and influence, that the institution in which Chomsky carries out his research into the structure of language and the properties of the human mind should be that citadel of modern science, the Massachusetts Institute of Technology, but that the views he expresses in summarizing his research should be those more characteristic of the humanities departments of a traditional university. The contradiction is only apparent. For Chomsky's work suggests that the conventional boundary that exists between "arts" and "science" can, and should, be abolished.

Modern Linguistics: Aims and Attitudes

● ●

11

For many readers of this book, possibly the majority, linguistics will be a completely new subject. I shall begin, therefore, by explaining in very general terms what linguistics is. We can then move on, in the next chapter, to consider those aspects of the subject which have been of particular importance in the formation of Chomsky's own thought.

Linguistics is commonly defined as the science of language. The word "science" is crucial here, and in our discussion of Chomsky's work we shall be very concerned with the implications of this term. For the moment, however, we may say that a *scientific* description is one that is carried out systematically on the basis of objectively verifiable observations and within the framework of some general theory appropriate to the data. It is often said that linguistics properly so called is of relatively recent origin and that the investigation of language as practiced in Europe and America before the nineteenth century was subjective, speculative, and unsystematic. Whether this sweeping condemnation of past linguistic research is historically justifiable is a question that we need not go into here. The important point to note is that linguistics as we know it today was developed in conscious opposition to the more traditional approaches to the study of language characteristic of earlier centuries. As we shall see, this deliberate break with the past was sharper and more definitive in America than it was in Europe. Nowhere was the rejection of traditional grammar more vehemently expressed than by the "Bloomfieldian" school of linguistics, dominant in the United States in the years following the Second World War—the school in which Chomsky was trained and against which, in due course, he reacted.

We shall not discuss here all the characteristics of modern linguistics that distinguish it from traditional grammar, but only those that are relevant to the theme of this book. The first of these, which is often regarded as a direct consequence of the scientific status of linguistics, is its *autonomy*, or independence of other disciplines. Traditional grammar, which like so much else in Western culture originated in Greece in the fifth century B.C., has since its beginnings been intimately connected with philosophy and literary criticism. At various times either the literary or the philosophical influence has been predominant, but they have both been present to some degree in all periods, and together they have shaped the attitudes and presuppositions with which scholars have for centuries approached the study of language. It is worth remembering also that these attitudes and presuppositions are now so pervasive and so deeply entrenched in our culture that not only the scholar trained in traditional grammar, but also the man in the street, tends to accept them without question. When the linguist claims "autonomy" for his subject he is asking to be allowed to take a fresh and objective look at language without prior commitment to traditional ideas and without necessarily adopting the same point of view as philosophers, psychologists, literary critics, or representatives of other disciplines. This does not mean that there is not, or should not be, any connection between linguistics and other disciplines concerned with language. Indeed, as we shall see in the later chapters of this book, there is at the present time a remarkable convergence of interest among linguists, psychologists, and philosophers. But the present *rapprochement* has come about as a consequence of the development of "autonomous" linguistics; and it is linguistics (more particularly, the work of Chomsky) that has provided the inspiration for the alliance of the three disciplines.

Reference has been made earlier to the literary bias of traditional grammar. That bias, which derived from the fact that the earliest Western grammarians were mainly concerned with the preservation and interpretation of the texts of the classical Greek writers, manifested itself in various ways. Scholars tended to concentrate upon the written language and to ignore the difference between speech and writing. Although the spoken language was not entirely neglected by traditional grammarians, it was only too often regarded as an imperfect copy of the written language. By contrast, most linguists today take it as axiomatic that speech is primary and that the written language is secondary and derived from it: in other words, that sound (more particularly, the range of sounds that can be produced by the so-called "speech organs") is the *medium* in which language is "embodied" and that written languages result from the transference of speech to a secondary, visual medium. Every known language existed first as a spoken language, and thousands of languages have never, or only very recently, been committed to writing. Furthermore, children acquire a command of the spoken language before they learn to read and write; they do so spontaneously, without any training, whereas reading and writing are special skills in which the child is normally given special instruction based upon his prior knowledge of the corresponding spoken language. Although nothing will be said about phonetics in this book, and all the illustrative material will be cited in its normal written form, it must be constantly borne in mind that we are mainly concerned with the spoken language.

It should be emphasized that adherence to the principle of the primacy of speech over writing does not imply a lack of interest in, still less a contempt for, written languages. Nor does it necessarily imply (although many linguists, it must be admitted, have failed to make this qualification) that the written language is wholly derivative. The conditions in which the written language is used are different from the conditions in which the spoken language is employed: since there is no face-to-face confrontation of reader and writer, information that is normally carried by the gestures and facial expressions accompanying speech and by a complex of other features that we may subsume here under the impressionistic term "tone of voice" must be conveyed in writing, if at all, by other means. The conventions of punctuation and the practice of italicizing words for emphasis are incapable of representing all the significant variations of pitch and stress that are present in spoken utterance. There will always be some degree of independence, therefore, in the written language. In many instances, as in the case of English, the difference between the spoken and the written forms of the "same" language has been increased by the conservatism of the orthographic conventions, established some centuries ago and maintained to this day despite the changes that have since taken place in the pronounciation of the language in different parts of the world.

One further point should be made in this connection. It is often said that none of the "speech organs" has as its sole, or indeed its primary, function the part it plays in the production of speech—that the lungs are used in breathing, the teeth in the mastication of food, and so on—and that the "speech organs" do not constitute a physiological system in the normal sense of this term. It should not be forgotten, however, that the faculty of speech is as characteristic of human beings, and as natural and important to them, as walking on two feet, or even eating. Whatever may have been the cause of this, in some remote period of man's evolutionary development, it is a fact to be accounted for that all human beings make use of the same physiological "apparatus" in speech. It is at least conceivable that they are genetically "programed" to do so. The relevance of this point to the ideas of Chomsky will become clear in a later chapter.

Traditional grammarians were concerned more or less exclusively with the standard literary language; and they tended to disregard, or to condemn as "incorrect," informal or colloquial usage in both speech and writing. Also, they often failed to realize that the standard language was, from a historical point of view, merely that regional or social dialect that had acquired prestige and become the instrument of administration, education, and literature. Because of its more widespread use by a greater number of people and for a wider range of activities, the standard language may have acquired a richer vocabulary than any of the co-existent "substandard" dialects, but this has not made it intrinsically more correct.

The distinction between "language" and "dialect" is commonly drawn on political grounds. There is less difference between Swedish, Danish, and Norwegian, for example, which are usually referred to as distinct "languages," than there is between many of the so-called "dialects" of Chinese. The important point is that the regional or social dialects of a language, say English, are no less systematic than the standard language and should not be described as imperfect approximations to it. This point is worth emphasizing, since many people are inclined to believe that it is only the standard language taught in school that is subject to systematic description. From a purely linguistic point of view, all the dialects of English are worthy of equal consideration.

Traditional grammar was developed on the basis of

Greek and Latin, and it was subsequently applied, with minimal modifications and often uncritically, to the description of a large number of other languages. But there are many languages that, in certain respects at least, are strikingly different in structure from Latin, Greek, and the more familiar languages of Europe and Asia. One of the principal aims of modern linguistics has therefore been to construct a theory of grammar that is more *general* than the traditional theory—one that is appropriate for the description of all human languages and is not biased in favor of those languages which are similar in their grammatical structure to Greek and Latin.

One should perhaps mention at this point that linguistics provides no support for those who believe that there is a fundamental difference between "civilized" and "primitive" languages. The vocabulary of a language will, of course, reflect the characteristic pursuits and interests of the society that uses it. Any of the major world languages—English, French, Russian—will have a large number of words relating to modern science and technology that will have no equivalent in the language of some "underdeveloped" people. Conversely, however, there will be many words in the language of, let us say, some remote and backward tribe in New Guinea or South America that cannot be translated satisfactorily into English, French, or Russian, because these are words that refer to objects, flora, fauna, or customs unfamiliar in Western culture. The vocabulary of one language cannot be described as richer or poorer than the vocabulary of some other language in any absolute sense; every language has a sufficiently rich vocabulary

for the expression of all the distinctions that are important in the society using it. We cannot therefore say,
from this point of view, that one language is more
"primitive" or more "advanced" than another. The point
is even clearer with respect to the grammatical structure
of languages. Differences there are between any particular "primitive" language and any particular "civilized"
language. But these are no greater on the average than
the differences between any random pair of "primitive"
languages and any random pair of "civilized" languages.
So-called "primitive" languages are no less systematic,
and are neither structurally simpler nor structurally
more complex, than the languages spoken by more
"civilized" peoples. This is an important point. All human societies of which we have knowledge speak languages of roughly equal complexity; and the differences
of grammatical structure that we do find among languages throughout the world are such that they cannot
be correlated with the cultural development of the people
speaking them and cannot be used as evidence for the
construction of an evolutionary theory of human language. The uniqueness of language to the human species
and the fact that no languages seem to be more primitive
than any others, or closer to systems of animal communication, are points that have been given particular
prominence in Chomsky's more recent work.

What are the features of human languages, then,
that distinguish them from the systems of communication used by other species? This question will occupy
us in greater detail later, but two particularly striking
properties of human language may be mentioned here.
The first of these is *duality of structure.* Every language

so far investigated (and we may confidently assume that this will also be true of any language yet to come to the attention of linguists) has two *levels* of grammatical structure. There is, first of all, what we may call the "primary," or *syntactic,* level of analysis, at which sentences can be represented as combinations of meaningful units: we will call these *words* (and gloss over the fact that not all the minimal syntactic units in all languages are words in the usual sense of this term). And there is also a "secondary," or *phonological,* level, at which sentences can be represented as combinations of units which are themselves without meaning and serve for the identification of the "primary" units. The "secondary" units of language are sounds, or *phonemes* (to use a more technical term). If we take as an example the sentence *He went to London* (and, purely for the purpose of exposition, make the simplifying assumption that each letter represents one and only one phoneme), we can say that the sentence is composed of four words and that the first of these "primary" units is identified by the combination of the "secondary" units *h* and *e* (in that order), the second of the "primary" units by the combination *w, e, n,* and *t,* and so on. It should be noted that there is nothing that is particularly novel in the principle of duality of structure, as I have described it here. It was recognized in traditional grammar. But one point should be stressed. Although I have said that the "primary" units, unlike the "secondary" units, convey meaning (and this, in general at least, is true), it is not the defining characteristic of words that they have meaning. As we shall see, it is possible to analyze language at the syntactic level without reference to whether the units established at this level have meaning or not; and there are some words at least that have no meaning (e.g., *to* in *I want to go home*). We must be careful, therefore, not to describe the duality of structure that is being referred to here in terms of the association of sound and meaning.

Granted that every language manifests the property of duality of structure, we may expect that the description, or *grammar,* of every language will consist of three interrelated parts. The part that accounts for the regularities governing the combination of words is *syntax.* It is by means of syntactic rules, for example, that we specify that *He went to London*, by contrast with **Went to he London*,[1] is a grammatical sentence. That part of grammar which describes the meaning of words and sentences is *semantics.* And the part of grammar that deals with the sounds and their permissible combinations (e.g., the fact that *went*, but not **twne*, is a possible English word) is *phonology.*

At this point I should perhaps warn the reader that there is a certain amount of terminological confusion and inconsistency in linguistics. In the previous paragraph I have used the term "grammar" to refer to the whole of the systematic description of language, including both phonology and semantics, as well as syntax. This is the sense in which Chomsky uses the word "grammar" in his more recent writings; and I shall adhere to this usage throughout the present book, except in those sections where I explicitly draw the reader's

---

[1] The asterisk prefixed here indicates that this sequence of words is ungrammatical. We shall use this standard notational convention throughout.

attention to the fact that I am employing the term in a somewhat narrower sense. Many linguists describe as "grammar" what I am calling "syntax" and give a correspondingly restricted interpretation to "syntax" (opposing it to "morphology"). There are certain points of substance involved in the choice of terminology. But we need not go into these in this brief, and necessarily somewhat superficial, account of the aims and attitudes of modern linguistics. In this book we shall be mainly concerned with the theory of syntax, since this is the field where Chomsky has made his major contribution to the more technical side of linguistics.

The second general property of human language to be mentioned here is its *creativity* (or "open-endedness"). By this is meant the capacity that all native speakers of a language have to produce and understand an indefinitely large number of sentences that they have never heard before and that may indeed never have been uttered before by anyone. The native speaker's "creative" command of his language, it should be noted, is in normal circumstances unconscious and unreflecting. He is generally unaware of applying any grammatical rules or systematic principles of formation when he constructs either new sentences or sentences he has previously encountered. And yet the sentences that he utters will generally be accepted by other native speakers of the language as correct and will be understood by them. (We must make allowances, as we shall see later, for a certain amount of error—hence the qualification implied by "generally" in the previous sentence—but this does not affect the principle that is under discussion here.) As far as we know, this creative command of language is unique to human beings: it is *species-spe-cific*. Systems of communication employed by species other than man are not "open-ended" in the same way. Most of them are "closed," in the sense that they admit of the transmission of only a finite and relatively small set of distinct "messages," the "meanings" of which are fixed (rather as the messages that one may send by means of the international telegraphic code are determined in advance), and it is not possible for the animal to vary these and construct new "sentences." It is true that certain forms of animal communication (for example, the signaling "code" that is used by bees to indicate the direction and distance of a source of honey) incorporate the possibility of making new "sentences" by systematically varying the "signal." But in all instances there is a simple correlation between the two variables—the "signal" and its "meaning." For example, as K. von Frisch discovered in his celebrated work on the subject, it is by the intensity of their body movements that bees signal the distance of the source of honey from the hive; and this parameter of "intensity" is subject to infinite (and continuous) variation. This kind of continuous variation is also found in human language: for instance, one can vary the "intensity" with which the word *very* is pronounced in a sentence like *He was very rich.* But it is not this feature that is being referred to when one talks of the creativity of human language. It is the ability to construct new combinations of discrete units, rather than simply to vary continuously one of the parameters of the signaling system in accordance with a correspondingly continuous variation in the "meaning" of the "messages." As we shall see in due course, Chomsky considers that the creativity of language is one of its most characteristic features and one that poses a particularly challenging problem for the development of a psychological theory of language use and language acquisition.

We have now introduced a number of the more important general principles that we shall take for granted, even when we do not draw explicitly upon them, in the following chapters. It may be helpful if I summarize them here. Modern linguistics claims to be more scientific and more general than traditional grammar. It assumes that the "natural" medium for the expression of language is sound (as produced by the speech organs) and that written languages are derived from speech. The grammar of any language will comprise at least the following three interrelated parts: syntax, semantics, and phonology; and it should, among other things, account for the ability native speakers have to produce and understand an indefinitely large number of "new" sentences.

What has been said in this chapter (due allowance being made for differences of emphasis) is neutral with respect to the theoretical differences that divide one school of linguistics from another at the present time. We now turn to a discussion of the "Bloomfieldian" (and "post-Bloomfieldian" or "neo-Bloomfieldian") school, in which, as I have said, Chomsky received his first training in linguistics.

The "Bloomfieldians"

● ● ●

111

Linguistics in the United States has been very strongly influenced in this century by the necessity of describing as many as possible of the hundreds of previously unrecorded languages existing in North America. Since the publication of the *Handbook of American Indian Languages* in 1911, almost every linguist in America has, until very recently, included some original research on one or more of the American Indian languages as part of his training; and many of the features characteristic of American linguistics can be, in part at least, explained by this fact.

First of all, the experience of working with the indigenous languages of North America has given to a good deal of American linguistic theory its practical character and its sense of urgency. Many of these languages were spoken by very few people and would soon die out. Unless they were recorded and described before this happened, they would become forever inaccessible to investigation. In these circumstances, it is not surprising that American linguists have given considerable attention to the development of what are called "field methods"—techniques for the recording and analysis of languages that the linguist himself could not speak and that had not previously been committed to writing. There were no doubt other relevant factors (in particular, a certain interpretation of scientific rigor and objectivity), but the fact that linguistic theory was for many American scholars no more than a source of techniques for the description of previously unrecorded languages was at least partly to blame for what Chomsky was to condemn later as its concern with "discovery procedures."

Franz Boas (1858–1942), who wrote the Introduction to the *Handbook of American Indian Languages* (1911) and gave there an outline of the method he had himself worked out for their systematic description, came to the conclusion that the range of variation to be found in human languages was far greater than one might suppose if one based one's generalizations upon the grammatical descriptions of the more familiar languages of Europe. He found that earlier descriptions of the indigenous and "exotic" languages of the North American subcontinent had been distorted by the failure of linguists to appreciate the potential diversity of languages and their attempt to impose the traditional grammatical categories of description upon languages for which these were wholly inappropriate; and he pointed out that none of these traditional categories was necessarily present in all languages. To use two of Boas's examples: the distinction between singular and plural is not obligatory in Kwakiutl, so that *There is a house over there* and *There are some houses over there* are not necessarily distinguished; and the distinction between present and past tense is not made in Eskimo (*The man is coming* vs. *The man was coming*). Boas also gave examples of the converse situation, grammatical distinctions that were obligatory in certain American Indian languages but that were given no place at all in traditional grammatical theory: "Some of the Siouan languages classify nouns by means of particles, and strict distinctions are made between animate moving and animate at rest, animate long, inanimate high and inanimate collective objects." Examples like this were used by Boas to support the view that every language has its own unique grammatical structure and that the task of the linguist is to discover for each language the categories of description appropriate to it. This view may be called "structuralist" (in one of the many senses of a rather fashionable term).

It should be stressed that the "structuralist" approach was by no means confined to Boas and his successors in America. Similar views had been expressed by Wilhelm von Humboldt (1767–1835); and they were also expressed by European contemporaries of Boas, who were experienced, as he was, in the description of "exotic" languages. "Structuralism" has in fact been the rallying cry of many different twentieth-century schools of linguistics.

It would be universally agreed that the two greatest and most influential figures in American linguistics after

Boas, in the period from the foundation of the Linguistic Society of America in 1924 to the beginning of the Second World War, were Edward Sapir (1884–1939) and Leonard Bloomfield (1887–1949). They were very different in temperament, in the range of their interests, in philosophical persuasion, and in the nature of the influence they exerted. Sapir had been trained in Germanic philology; but, while he was still a student, he came under the influence of Boas and turned to the study of American Indian languages. Like Boas, and like many American scholars down to the present day, he was an anthropologist as well as a linguist, and published widely in both fields. But Sapir's interests and professional competence extended beyond anthropology and linguistics, into literature, music, and art. He published a large number of articles and reviews (dealing with very many different languages), but only one book. This was a relatively short work, called *Language*, which appeared in 1921 and was addressed to the general reader. It is strikingly different, both in content and in style, from Bloomfield's *Language*, published twelve years later.

Bloomfield, as we shall see, did more than anyone else to make linguistics autonomous and scientific (as he understood the term "scientific"); and in the pursuit of this aim he was prepared to restrict the scope of the subject, excluding from consideration many aspects of language which, he believed, could not yet be treated with sufficient precision and rigor. Sapir, as one might expect from his other interests, took a more "humanistic" view of language. He laid great stress on its cultural importance, on the priority of reason over volition and emotion (emphasizing what he called "the prevailing cognitive character" of language), and on the fact that language was "purely human" and "non-instinctive."

Sapir's *Language*, though far shorter, is much more general and is easier to read (at a superficial level at least) than Bloomfield's. It is packed with brilliant analogies and suggestive comparisons, but Sapir's refusal to neglect any of the multifarious aspects of language gives to many of his theoretical statements, it must be admitted, an aura of vagueness that is absent from Bloomfield's book. Sapir's work has continued to hold the attention of linguists down to the present day. But there never has been a "Sapirian" school in the sense in which there has been, and still is, a "Bloomfieldian" school of linguistics in America. It is not surprising that this should be so. We shall say no more about Sapir, except to point out that many of the attitudes toward language that Sapir held are now held by Chomsky, although Chomsky's ideas have been developed in the "Bloomfieldian" tradition of "autonomous" linguistics.

As Bloomfield understood the term "scientific" (and this was a fairly common interpretation at the time), it implied the deliberate rejection of all data that were not directly observable or physically measurable. J. B. Watson, founder of the so-called "behaviorist" approach in psychology, took the same view of the aims and methodology of science. According to Watson and his followers, psychologists had no need to postulate the existence of the mind or of anything else that was not observable in order to explain those activities and capacities of human beings that were traditionally described as "mental" or "rational." The behavior of any organism, from an amoeba to a human being, was to be described and explained in terms of the organism's *response* to the *stimuli* presented by features of the environment. It was assumed that the organism's learning of these responses could be explained satisfactorily by means of the familiar laws of physics and chemistry, in much the same way as one might explain how a thermostat "learns" to respond to changes in temperature and to switch a furnace on or off.[1] Speech was but one among a number of forms of overt, or directly observable, behavior characteristic of human beings; and thought was merely inaudible speech ("talking with concealed musculature," as Watson put it). Since inaudible speech could be made audible, when necessary, thought was in principle a form of observable behavior.

When Bloomfield came to write his monumental book *Language*, he explicitly adopted behaviorism as a framework for linguistic description.[2] In the second chapter he contrasted the traditional "mentalistic" explanation of language with "the *materialistic* (or, better, mechanistic) theory," according to which "human actions . . . are part of cause-and-effect sequences exactly like those we observe, say, in the study of physics or chemistry." He went on to claim that, although we could, in prin-

[1] John Marshall has informed me that it is debatable whether the early behaviorists held such an extreme view as this. He suggests that Bloomfield's behaviorism was more radical than that of many of the psychologists who influenced him because he was himself a "convert" from mentalism. For a discussion of the historical background from this point of view, the reader is referred to Marshall's review of Esper's *Mentalism and Objectivism in Linguistics*.
[2] He had no less explicitly declared his adherence to the "mentalistic" psychology of Wundt in his earlier work, *An Introduction to the Study of Language*.

ciple, foretell whether a certain stimulus would cause someone to speak and, if so, exactly what he would say, in practice we could make the prediction "only if we knew the exact structure of his body at the moment."[3] The meaning of a linguistic form was defined as "the practical events" with which the form "is connected," and, in a later chapter, as "the situation in which the speaker utters it and the response which it calls forth in the hearer."[4] As an example of a simple, but presumably typical, situation in which language might be used, Bloomfield suggested the following: Jack and Jill are walking down a lane; Jill sees an apple on a tree and, being hungry, asks Jack to get it for her; he climbs the tree and gives her the apple; and she eats it. This is the way in which we would normally describe the events that take place. A behavioristic account would run somewhat differently: Jill's being hungry ("that is, some of her muscles were contracting, and some fluids were being secreted, especially in her stomach") and her seeing the apple (that is, light waves reflected from the apple reached her eyes) constitute the stimulus. The more direct response to this stimulus would be for Jill to climb the tree and get the apple herself. Instead, she makes a "substitute response" in the form of a particular sequence of noises with her speech organs; and this acts as a "substitute stimulus" for Jack, causing him to act as he might have done if he himself had been hungry and had seen the apple.

This behavioristic analysis of the situation obviously leaves a lot to be explained, but we shall not stop to

[3] Bloomfield, *Language*, p. 33.
[4] *Ibid.*, pp. 27, 139.

discuss this question at this point. Bloomfield's fable will give the reader some idea of the way in which language was held to operate in practical situations as a substitute for other kinds of non-symbolic behavior; and this is sufficient for our present purpose.

Bloomfield's commitment to behaviorism had no appreciable effect upon syntax or phonology in his own work or in that of his followers (except in so far as it fostered the development of an "empiricist" methodology: we shall come to this in due course). Bloomfield himself made reference to the behaviorist point of view only when he was dealing with meaning; and what he had to say on this topic was not calculated to inspire his followers with the desire to set about the construction of a comprehensive theory of semantics. It was Bloomfield's view that the analysis of meaning was "the weak point in language study" and that it would continue to be so "until human knowledge advances very far beyond its present state."[5] The reason for his pessimism lay in his conviction that a precise definition of the meaning of words presupposes a complete "scientific" description of the objects, states, processes, etc., to which they refer (i.e., for which they operate as "substitutes"). For a small number of words (the names of plants, animals, various natural substances, etc.) we were already in a position to give a reasonably precise definition by means of the technical terms of the relevant branch of science (botany, zoology, chemistry, etc.). But for the vast majority of words (Bloomfield gave examples like *love* and *hate*) this was not so. Bloomfield's attitude could not but discourage linguists

[5] *Ibid.*, p. 140.

from the study of meaning; and neither he nor his followers made any positive contribution whatsoever to the theory or practice of semantics. In fact, for almost thirty years after the publication of his book the study of meaning was wholly neglected by the "Bloomfieldian" school, and was frequently defined to be outside linguistics properly so called.

The "Bloomfieldian" attitude toward meaning, though stultifying as far as any progress in semantics was concerned, was not wholly detrimental to the development of other branches of linguistic theory. Bloomfield himself never suggested that it was possible to describe the syntax and phonology of a language in total ignorance of the meaning of words and sentences (although there can be little doubt that he would have thought this very desirable, if it were possible). His view was that for phonological and syntactic analysis it was necessary to know "whether two uttered forms were 'the same' or 'different,' " but that for this purpose all that was necessary was a rough-and-ready account of the meaning of words and not a full scientific description. Semantic considerations were strictly subordinated to the task of identifying the units of phonology and syntax and were not involved at all in the specification of the rules or principles governing their permissible combinations. This part of the grammar was to be a purely *formal* study, independent of semantics.

Bloomfield's followers carried even further than he did the attempt to formulate the principles of phonological and syntactic analysis without reference to meaning. This effort reached its culmination in the work of Zellig Harris, notably in his *Methods in Structural Linguistics,* first published in 1951, though completed some years before. Harris's work also constituted the most ambitious and the most rigorous attempt that had yet been made to establish what Chomsky was later to describe as a set of "discovery procedures" for grammatical description.

Chomsky was one of Harris's pupils and later one of his collaborators and colleagues, and his earliest publications are very similar in spirit to those of Harris. By 1957, when Chomsky's first book, *Syntactic Structures,* was published, he had already moved away, as we shall see, from the position that Harris and the other "Bloomfieldians" had adopted on the question of "discovery procedures." But Chomsky continued to maintain that the phonology and syntax of a language could, and should, be described as a purely formal system without reference to semantic considerations. Language was an instrument for the expression of meaning: it was both possible and desirable to describe this instrument, in the first instance at least, without drawing upon one's knowledge of the use to which it was put. Semantics was part of the description of the use of language; it was secondary to and dependent upon syntax, and outside linguistics proper. In recent years Chomsky has become increasingly critical of "Bloomfieldian" linguistics and has abandoned many of the assumptions he originally held. It is worth emphasizing, therefore, not only that his earlier views were formed in the "Bloomfieldian" school, but also that he could hardly have made the technical advances he did make in linguistics if the ground had not been prepared for him by such scholars as Harris.

The Goals of Linguistic Theory

IV

Before we move on to consider Chomsky's more technical contributions to linguistics, it will be as well to introduce and explain the motives and methodological assumptions that underlie his work. We shall concentrate mainly in this chapter on the account that Chomsky himself gives in his short but epoch-making book *Syntactic Structures*, published in 1957. As we shall see in due course, he takes a more comprehensive view of the scope of linguistics in his later works. Chapter 6 of *Syntactic Structures* bears the title "On the Goals of Linguistic Theory," which I have borrowed for my own chapter.

As I have already said, Chomsky's general views on linguistic theory as presented in *Syntactic Structures* are in most respects the same as those held by other members of the "Bloomfieldian" school, notably by Zellig Harris. In particular, it may be noted that there is no hint, at this period, of the "rationalism" that is so characteristic a feature of Chomsky's more recent writing. His acknowledgment of the influence of the "empiricist" philosophers, Goodman and Quine, would suggest that he shared their views; but there is no general discussion, in *Syntactic Structures*, of the philosophical and psychological implications of grammar.

However, there are one or two points that sharply distinguish even Chomsky's earlier work from that of Harris and the other "Bloomfieldians." In Chapter II, I mentioned that Chomsky lays great stress on the *creativity* (or "open-endedness") of human language and claims that the theory of grammar should reflect the ability that all fluent speakers of a language possess to produce and understand sentences they have never heard before. As Chomsky came to realize later, earlier scholars, including Wilhelm von Humboldt and Ferdinand de Saussure (1857–1913), had also insisted upon the importance of this property of creativity. Actually, it had been taken for granted, and occasionally mentioned explicitly, since the very beginnings of Western linguistic theory in the ancient world. But it had been neglected, if not denied, in "Bloomfieldian" formulations of the aims of linguistic theory. The reason for this seems to have been that the "Bloomfieldians," in common with many other twentieth-century schools of linguistics, were very conscious of the need to distinguish clearly between *descriptive* and *prescriptive* (or *normative*) grammar: between the description of the rules that are actually followed by native speakers and the prescription of rules that, in the opinion of the grammarian, they ought to follow, in order to speak "correctly." There are many examples of prescriptive rules set up by grammarians that have no basis in the normal usage of native speakers of English. (One such instance is the rule that says that *It is I*, rather than the more usual *It's me*, is "correct" English.) So concerned were the "Bloomfieldians" (and various other "schools") with asserting the status of linguistics as a descriptive science that they made it a point of principle not to venture any judgments about the grammaticality, or "correctness," of sentences, unless these sentences had been attested in the usage of native speakers and included in the corpus of material that formed the basis of the grammatical description.

Chomsky insisted that the vast majority of the sentences in any representative corpus of recorded utterances would be "new" sentences, in the sense that they would occur once, and once only; and that this would remain true however long we went on recording utterances made by native speakers. The English language, like all the natural languages, consists of an indefinitely large number of sentences, only a small fraction of which have ever been uttered or will ever be uttered. The grammatical description of English may be based upon a corpus of actually attested utterances, but it will describe these, and classify them as "grammatical," only incidentally as it were, by "projecting" them onto the indefinitely large set of sentences that constitutes the language. Using Chomsky's terminology, we shall say that the grammar *generates* (and thereby defines as "grammatical") all the sentences of the language and does not distinguish between those that have been attested and those that have not.

The distinction that Chomsky draws in *Syntactic Structures* between the sentences generated by the grammar (the *language*) and a sample of the utterances produced, in normal conditions of use, by native speakers (the *corpus*), he draws in his later writings in terms of the notions of *competence* and *performance*. This terminological change is symptomatic of the evolution in Chomsky's thought from empiricism to rationalism, which has already been mentioned and will be discussed more fully later. In his later works, though not in *Syntactic Structures*, he stresses the fact that many of the utterances produced by native speakers (samples of their "performance") will, for various reasons, be ungrammatical. These reasons have to do with such linguistically irrelevant factors as lapses of memory or attention and malfunctions of the psychological mechanisms underlying speech. Given that this is so, it follows that the linguist cannot take the corpus of attested utterances at its face value, as part of the language to be generated by the grammar. He must *idealize* the "raw data" to some degree and eliminate from the corpus all those utterances which the native speaker would recognize, by virtue of his "competence," as ungrammatical. At first sight it might appear that Chomsky is here guilty of the confusion between description and prescription that was so common in traditional grammar. But this is not so. The view that all the utterances of a native speaker of a language are equally correct, and are proved to be so by the sole fact of their having been uttered—although it is a view that has often been maintained by linguists of an empiricist bent—is in the last resort untenable. And Chomsky is clearly right to claim for linguistics the same right to disregard some of the "raw data" as is accepted as normal in other sciences. There are, of course, serious problems, both practical and theoretical, involved in deciding what constitute extraneous or linguistically irrelevant factors; and it may well be that, in practice, the "idealization" of the data advocated by Chomsky does tend to introduce some of the normative considerations that marred much of traditional grammar. But this does not affect the general principle.

A further and related difference between Chomsky's earlier and later view of the "goals of linguistics" has to do with the role he assigns to the *intuitions*, or judgments, of native speakers. In *Syntactic Structures* he says that the sentences generated by the grammar should be "acceptable to the native speaker";[1] and he considers that it is a point in favor of the kind of grammar he develops that it also accounts for the "intuitions" of native speakers with respect to the way certain sentences are recognized as equivalent or ambiguous. But the intuitions of the native speaker are presented as independent evidence, and their explanation is regarded as being secondary to the principal task of generating the sentences of the language. In later work Chomsky includes the intuitions of the speakers of a language as part of the data to be accounted for by the grammar. Furthermore, he now seems to place more reliance upon

[1] Chomsky, *Syntactic Structures*, pp. 49–50.

the validity and reliability of these intuitions than he did earlier, when he was much concerned with the need to test them by means of satisfactory "operational" techniques.

As we saw in the previous chapter, American linguistics in the "Bloomfieldian" period tended to be very "procedural" in orientation. Questions of theory were reformulated as questions of method ("How should one go about the practical task of analyzing a language?"); and it was commonly assumed that it should be possible to develop a set of procedures which, when applied to a corpus of material in an unknown language (or a language treated as if it were unknown to the linguist), would yield the correct grammatical analysis of the language of which the corpus was a representative sample. One of the main points argued by Chomsky in *Syntactic Structures* is that this is an unnecessary, and indeed harmful, assumption: "a linguistic theory should not be identified with a manual of useful procedures, nor should it be expected to provide mechanical procedures for the discovery of grammars."[2] The means by which a linguist arrives, in practice, at one analysis rather than another might include "intuition, guess work, all sorts of partial methodological hints, reliance on past experience, etc."[3] What counts is the result; and this can be presented and justified without reference to the procedures that have been followed to achieve it. This does not mean that there is no point in trying to develop heuristic techniques for the description of lan-

[2] *Ibid.*, p. 55, fn. 6.
[3] *Ibid.*, p. 56.

guages, but simply—to put it crudely—that the proof of the pudding is in the eating. Just as the proof of a mathematical theorem can be checked without taking account of the way in which the person constructing the proof happened to hit upon the relevant intermediate propositions, so it should be with respect to grammatical analysis. As Chomsky says, the point would be granted immediately in the physical sciences, and there is no need for linguistics to set its sights higher than they do; especially as no linguist has yet come anywhere near formulating any satisfactory *discovery procedures*.

Linguistic theory should be concerned, then, with the justification of grammars. Chomsky goes on to consider the possibility of formulating criteria for deciding whether a particular grammar is the best one possible for the data. He concludes that even this goal—the formulation of a *decision procedure*—is too ambitious. The most that can be expected is that linguistic theory should provide criteria (an *evaluation procedure*) for choosing between alternative grammars. In other words, we cannot hope to say whether a particular description of the data is correct, in any absolute sense, but only that it is more correct than some alternative description of the same data.

Chomsky's distinction between decision procedures and evaluation procedures has caused a lot of misunderstanding and unnecessary controversy. After all, no physicist would say that Einstein's Theory of Relativity, for example, gives the best possible explanation of the data it covers, but only that it is better than the alternative theory, based on Newtonian physics, which it supplanted. Once again, why should linguistics set its sights higher than other sciences do? It is sometimes said that Chomsky's formulation of the goals of linguistic theory in terms of the comparison of alternative grammars glosses over the fact that for many languages we do not possess even a partial grammar and for no language do we have a grammar that is anywhere near being complete. This is indeed a fact. But the conclusion, that it is premature in these circumstances to talk of comparing grammars, does not follow. The construction of a set of grammatical rules involves the linguist in making decisions to handle the data in one way rather than another. Even if the rules describe only some small part of the data, there must be, whether explicit or implicit, a comparison of alternatives. It is the task of linguistic theory, says Chomsky, to make the alternatives explicit and to formulate general principles for deciding between them.

One further point should be made. Although Chomsky is, in one sense, proposing that linguistic theory should, in renouncing the "Bloomfieldian" quest for "discovery procedures," set itself a more modest goal than previously, there is a sense also in which his theoretical proposals are incomparably more ambitious than those of his predecessors. Some years before the publication of *Syntactic Structures*, in his little-known paper on "Systems of Syntactic Analysis," Chomsky had tried to formulate with mathematical precision some of the procedures of grammatical analysis outlined in Harris's *Methods in Structural Linguistics*. He was convinced by this experience, and by his examination of other "careful proposals for the development of linguistic theory," that the works in question, though apparently concerned with the specification of discovery procedures, in fact yielded "no more than evaluation procedures for grammars."[4] Chomsky's most original, and probably his most enduring, contribution to linguistics is the mathematical rigor and precision with which he formalized the properties of alternative systems of grammatical description. A fuller consideration of this topic must wait for the following chapters. Here we shall mention only one or two more general points.

At the very beginning of *Syntactic Structures*, Chomsky talks of a grammar as "a device of some sort for producing the sentences of the language under analysis." Chomsky's use of such words as "device" and "produce" in this context has misled many readers into thinking that he conceives of the grammar of a language in terms of some electronic or mechanical model—some piece of "hardware"—that replicates the behavior of the speaker of a language when he utters a sentence. It should be emphasized that he has employed these terms because the particular branch of mathematics that he has drawn upon in his formalization of grammar also uses such terms as "device," or even "machine," in a perfectly abstract way without reference to the physical properties of any actual model that might implement the abstract "device." This point will become clearer in the next chapter.

It is unfortunate, however, that Chomsky has used the word "produce" in the passage just cited. It almost inevitably suggests that the grammatical structure of the language is being described from the point of view

[4] *Ibid.*, p. 52.

of the speaker rather than the listener; that the grammar describes the production, and not the reception, of speech. There is a sense, as we shall see, in which a grammar of the kind developed by Chomsky does "produce" sentences by the application of a sequence of rules. But Chomsky has continually warned us against identifying the "production" of sentences within the grammar with the production of sentences by the speaker of a language. The grammar is intended to be neutral as between production and reception, to a certain extent explaining both, but no more biased toward one than it is toward the other. Chomsky does not usually talk of the grammar as "producing" sentences. The term he customarily employs is "generate"; and this is the term that we used earlier in this chapter. But what exactly is meant by the word "generate" in this context?

We have already seen that a *generative* grammar is one that "projects" any given set of sentences upon the larger, and possibly infinite, set of sentences that constitute the language being described, and that it is this property of the grammar that reflects the creative aspect of human language. But "generative" for Chomsky has a second and equally important, if not more important, sense. This second sense, in which "generative" may be glossed as "explicit," implies that the rules of the grammar and the conditions under which they operate must be precisely specified. We can perhaps best illustrate what is meant by "generative" in this sense by means of a simple mathematical analogy (and Chomsky's use of the term "generate" does in fact derive from mathematical usage). Consider the following algebraic expression, or function: $2x + 3y - z$. Given that the variables

x, y, and z can each take as its value one of the integers, the expression will generate (in terms of the usual arithmetical operations) an infinite set of resultant values. For example, with $x = 3$, $y = 2$, and $z = 5$, the result is 7; with $x = 1$, $y = 3$, and $z = 21$, the result is -10; and so on. We can say therefore that 7, -10, etc., are in the set of values generated by the function in question. If someone else applies the rules of arithmetic and obtains a different result, we say that he has made a mistake. We do not say that the rules are indeterminate and leave room for doubt at any point as to how they should be applied. Chomsky's conception of the rules of grammar is similar. They should be as precisely specified—*formalized* is the technical term—as the rules of arithmetic are. If we go on to identify the rules of the grammar with the native speaker's linguistic *competence*, as Chomsky does in his later work, we can account for the occurrence of ungrammatical sentences, and also for the occasional inability of listeners to analyze perfectly grammatical sentences, in much the same way as we can account for differences obtained in the evaluation of a mathematical function. We say that they are due to errors of *performance*—errors made in the application of the rules.

According to Chomsky, the grammar of a language should generate "all and only" the sentences of the language. If the reader is puzzled by the addition of "and only" (which is a relatively trivial instance of the kind of precision that is encouraged by formalization), he need only reflect that, by setting up the grammar in such a way that it generates every combination of English words (and this would be a very simple grammar), one would be sure of generating all the sentences of the language. But most of the combinations would not be sentences. The addition of "and only" is therefore an important qualification.

The generation of all and only the sentences of English, or any other language, might seem to be impossibly ambitious. It must be remembered, however, that this represents an ideal, which, even if it is impossible of fulfillment, is a goal toward which the grammarian of any language should continually work; and one grammar can be evaluated as better than another if, all other things being equal, it approximates more closely to this ideal. It should also be stressed, although this may appear somewhat paradoxical, that one is not committed by the adoption of Chomsky's ideal of generating all and only the sentences of the language to the view that the distinction between grammatical and ungrammatical sequences of words is invariably clear-cut, so that it is always possible to decide whether a given sequence should or should not be generated by the grammar. Chomsky points out in *Syntactic Structures* that it is a commonplace of the philosophy of science that, if a theory is formulated in such a way that it covers the clear cases, the theory itself can be used to decide the unclear cases. He advocates the same approach in linguistics; and for Chomsky a generative grammar is a scientific theory. To take a simple example (it is not one of Chomsky's): there are many speakers of English who would reject the putative sentence *The house will have been being built* and others who would accept it as quite normal. Since the judgments of native speakers do not seem to vary systematically with the dialects they speak, let us grant that, for English as a whole, the status of putative sentences like this is indeterminate (by contrast with the definitely acceptable *The house will have been built, The house is being built, They will have been building the house,* etc., and the definitely unacceptable **The house can will be built,* etc.). Since we do not know in advance whether *The house will have been being built* is a grammatical sentence or not, we can formulate the rules of the grammar to include all the definitely acceptable sequences and to exclude all the definitely unacceptable sequences and then see whether these rules exclude or include such sentences as *The house will have been being built.* (Sentences of this kind are in fact generated, and thereby defined as grammatical, by the rules given for English in *Syntactic Structures.*)

In this chapter we have confined our attention, for the most part, to Chomsky's earlier views on the aims and methodology of linguistics; and I have suggested that, except for his emphasis on the importance of creativity and his rejection of discovery procedures, when he wrote *Syntactic Structures* he was still very much a "Bloomfieldian." I have said that the most important and original part of Chomsky's earlier work lies in his formalization of various systems of generative grammar; and the next three chapters will be devoted to an account of this topic. We shall then take up the discussion of his more recent contributions to the psychology and philosophy of language.

Generative Grammar: a Simple Model

V

Our discussion of the more technical part of Chomsky's work will be relatively informal and will not presuppose any special training in, or aptitude for, mathematics. However, a sufficient number of terms and concepts will be introduced to give the reader some idea of the flavor of generative grammar and to make it possible for him to appreciate its significance. It should be pointed out that Chomsky's own treatment of generative grammar in *Syntactic Structures*, and indeed in most of his more accessible publications, is also fairly informal. But it rests upon a considerable amount of highly technical research, which he carried out in the years preceding the publication of *Syntactic Structures*. Much of this has never been published in full, though it was described, in 1955, in a lengthy mimeographed monograph, "The Logical Structure of Linguistic Theory," which was made available to interested scholars and university libraries.

In this chapter we shall be dealing with a very simple formal system, the first of the "three models for the description of language" discussed by Chomsky in *Syntactic Structures* and elsewhere—one which he very quickly proved was insufficiently powerful for the syntactic analysis of English and other natural languages. We shall first introduce a number of terms and concepts that will be required, not only here, but also for the discussion of the more complex models of grammar in the next two chapters. Throughout these three chapters we shall assume an intuitive knowledge of at least some of the sentences of English that we should definitely wish to regard as well formed, or *grammatical*, and of at least some of the sequences of words that we should definitely wish to classify as ill formed, or *ungrammatical*. How we have come by this knowledge and how we might go about putting it to the test are important questions, but they are irrelevant to the formalization of linguistic description, which is our present concern.

We may begin by defining the *language* that is described by a particular grammar as the set of all the sentences it generates. The set of sentences may be, in principle, either finite or infinite in number. But English (and as far as we know all other natural languages) comprises an infinite (i.e., indefinitely large) number of sentences, because there are sentences and phrases in the language that can be extended indefinitely and will yet be accepted as perfectly normal by native speakers. Obvious examples are sentences like *This is the man that married the girl that* . . . (sentences of the "House-that-Jack-built" type) and phrases like *large, black, three-cornered . . . hat,* which can be expanded to any desired length by making appropriate insertions in place of the three dots. Obviously, there are certain practical limitations upon the length of any sentence that has ever been, or will ever be, uttered by native speakers of English. But the point is that no *definite* limit can be set to the length of English sentences. We must, therefore, accept that, in theory, the number of grammatical sentences in the language is infinite.

But the number of words in the vocabulary of English is, we will assume, finite. There is a considerable variation in the words known to different native speakers, and there may well be some difference between the "active" and the "passive" vocabulary of every individual (i.e., between the words he will himself use as a speaker and the words he will recognize and understand if someone else uses them). Indeed, neither the "active" nor the "passive" vocabulary of any native speaker of English is fixed and static even for relatively short periods of time. We shall, however, discount these facts in our discussion of the grammar of English and assume, for simplicity, that the vocabulary of the language is both determinate and invariable, and of course finite.

We shall also assume that the number of distinct operations that are involved in the generation of English sentences is finite in number. There is no reason to believe that this is an implausible assumption; and if they were not, this would mean that the sentences of English could not be generated by means of a specifiable set of rules. Now, if the grammar is to consist of a finite set of rules operating upon a finite vocabulary and is to be capable of generating an infinite set of sentences, it follows that at least some of the rules must be applicable more than once in the generation of the same sentence. Such rules, and the structures they generate, are called *recursive*. Once again, there is nothing implausible in the suggestion that the grammar of English should include a certain number of recursive rules. It is intuitively clear that in expanding the sentence *This is the man that married the girl* by adding to it the clause *that wrote the book*, a clause of the same type as *that married the girl* has been added to the original sentence.

Sentences can be represented, as we saw in Chapter II, at two *levels*: at the syntactic level as sequences of words and at the phonological level as sequences of phonemes. It would be possible, in principle, to consider the syntactic structure of sentences as something that is totally or partially independent of the order in which the words occur relative to one another; and certain languages, with what is described as "free word order," have been traditionally described from this point of view. However, following Chomsky, we shall make it a matter of definition that every different sequence of words (if it is well formed) is a different sentence. Under this definition, not only are *The dog bit the man* and *The man bit the dog* different sentences, but so also are *I had an idea on my way home* and *On my way home I had an idea*.

From the purely syntactic point of view, the phonological structure of words is irrelevant; and we could represent them in any one of a variety of ways. For instance, we could list all the words in the vocabulary in some arbitrary order, number them according to their place on the list, and then use these numbers to denote particular words in the syntactic description of sentences. It is the usual practice, however, to represent words as sequences of phonemes (or letters) even at the syntactic level; and we shall follow this practice. We shall, in fact, cite words and syntactic units in their normal orthographic form, but the reader should bear in mind that the spelling or pronunciation of words is, in principle, independent of their identity as syntactic units. It is generally accepted that two different words may be written or pronounced in the same way and that there can be alternative ways of spelling or pronouncing the same word.

We shall now introduce a distinction between "terminal" and "auxiliary" elements. *Terminal elements* are those which actually occur in sentences: words at the syntactic level and phonemes at the phonological level. All other terms or symbols that are employed in the formulation of grammatical rules may be described as *auxiliary elements.* In particular, it should be noted that the terms or symbols used to denote the "parts of speech" are auxiliary elements in generative grammars of the kind we shall be considering. We shall use familiar traditional terms for word classes, or "parts of speech," as Chomsky does, and abbreviate them symbolically: N = Noun, V = Verb, etc. Other auxiliary elements will be introduced later. One point that should be stressed here is that in a generative grammar the fact that a particular word belongs to a particular class—that it is a member of the class N, let us say—must be made perfectly explicit within the grammar. In effect this means, in grammars of the type formalized by Chomsky, that every word in the vocabulary must be assigned to the syntactic class, or classes, to which it belongs: it will not be sufficient to draw up a set of definitions, such as "A noun is the name of any person, place, or thing," and then leave it to the person referring to the grammar to decide whether a particular word satisfies the definition or not.

The simplest grammars discussed by Chomsky that are capable of generating an infinite set of sentences by means of a finite number of recursive rules operating upon a finite vocabulary are what he calls *finite-state grammars*. These are based on the view that sentences are generated by means of a series of choices made "from left to right": that is to say, after the first, or leftmost, element has been selected, every subsequent choice is determined by the immediately preceding elements. According to this conception of syntactic structure, a sentence like *This man has brought some bread* might be generated as follows. The word *this* would be selected for the first position from a list of all the words capable of occurring at the beginning of English sentences. Then *man* would be selected as one of the words possible after *this*; *has* as one of the words that can occur after *this* and *man*; and so on. If we had selected *that*, instead of *this*, for the first position, the subsequent choices would have been unaffected: *That man has brought some bread* is an equally acceptable sentence. On the other hand, if we had first selected *those* or *these*, we should then have to select words like *men* for the second position, followed by words like *have* for the third position—the possibilities for the fourth and subsequent positions being as before. And if we had selected *the* initially, we could continue with either *man* and *has* or *men* and *have*. One way of representing graphically what has just been said in words is by means of the "state diagram" shown in Figure 1 (I have deliberately used a slightly more complicated example than the one Chomsky gives on p. 19 of *Syntactic Structures*).

The diagram may be interpreted as follows. We can think of the grammar as a machine, or device (in the abstract sense explained in the previous chapter), which moves through a finite number of internal "states" as it passes from the *initial state* ("start") to the *final state* ("stop") in the generation of sentences. When it has produced (let us say, "printed out" or "emitted") a word (from the set of words given as possible for that "state") the grammar then "switches" to a new state as determined by the arrows. Any sequence of words that can be generated in this way is thereby defined to be grammatical (in terms of the grammar represented by the diagram).

The grammar illustrated in Figure 1 will generate, of course, only a finite number of sentences. It can be extended, however, by allowing the device to "loop" back to the same or some previous state at particular points of choice. For example, we could add "loops" between {*this, that, the, some, a, . . .*} and {*man, bread, book, . . .*} and between {*these, those, the, some, . . .*} and {*men, books, . . .*} making possible the selection of one or more elements from the set {*awful, fat, big, . . .*}, and thus the generation of sentences beginning *That awful man, That big fat man, Some big fat awful men*, etc. The grammar could also be extended in an obvious way to allow for the generation of compound sentences like

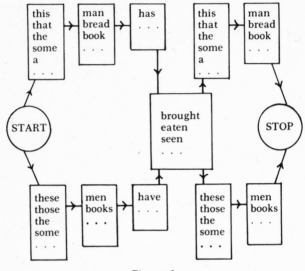

Figure 1

That man has brought us some bread and this beautiful girl has eaten the cheese.

These sentences are still very simple in structure; and it would clearly be a complicated matter, even if it were possible, to construct a finite-state grammar capable of generating a large and representative sample of the sentences of English. It will be observed, for example, that we have had to put *the* both with *this, that,* etc., and with *these, those,* etc. We would also have to put {*awful, fat, big,* ...} in several different places, because *this awful man* and *these awful men,* but not **these awful man* and **this awful men,* are acceptable. Problems of this kind would multiply very quickly if we seriously set about the task of writing a finite-state grammar for English; and the conception of syntactic structure that underlies this model of description has little to recommend it other than its formal simplicity. But Chomsky proved that our rejection of finite-state grammar as a satisfactory model for the description of natural language is more solidly based than it would be if it rested solely upon considerations of practical complexity and our intuitions as to how certain grammatical phenomena ought to be described. He demonstrated the inadequacy of finite-state grammars by pointing out that there are certain regular processes of sentence formation in English that cannot be accounted for at all, no matter how clumsy or counterintuitive an analysis we were prepared to tolerate, within the framework of finite-state grammar.

Chomsky's proof of the inadequacy of finite-state grammar[1] rests upon the fact that there may be dependencies holding between non-adjacent words and that these interdependent words may themselves be separated by a phrase or clause containing another pair of non-adjacent interdependent words. For example, in a sentence like *Anyone who says that is lying* there is a dependency between the words *anyone* and *is lying*. They are separated by the simple clause *who says that* (in which there is a dependency between *who* and *says*). We can easily construct more complex examples: e.g., *Anyone who says that people who deny that . . . are wrong is foolish.* Here we have dependencies between *anyone* and *is foolish*, and between *people* and

[1] Chomsky, *Syntactic Structures*, pp. 21–24.

are wrong; and we can go on to insert between *that* and *are* a clause which itself contains non-adjacent inter-dependent words. The result is a sentence with "mirror-image properties"—that is to say, a sentence of the form $a + b + c \ldots x + y + z$, where there is a relationship of compatibility or dependency between the outermost constituents (a and z), between the next outermost (b and y), and so on. Any language that contains an indefinitely large number of sentences with "mirror-image properties" like this is beyond the scope of finite-state grammar.

As I have said, the generation of sentences by means of a series of choices made "from left to right" has little to recommend it other than the formal simplicity of the model. The reason why Chomsky paid any attention at all to finite-state ·grammar is that language had been considered from this point of view in connection with the design of efficient channels of communication during the Second World War; and the highly sophisticated mathematical theory of communication that resulted ("information theory") was extended to many fields, including psychology and linguistics, after the war. Chomsky did not prove, or claim to prove, that "information theory," as such, was irrelevant to the investigation of language, but merely that, if it were applied on the assumption of "word-by-word" and "left-to-right" generation, it could not handle some of the constructions in English.

Phrase Structure Grammar

vi

In the previous chapter we made the tacit assumption that the syntactic structure of a sentence could be fully accounted for by specifying the words of which the sentence was composed and the order in which they occurred. We saw that a finite-state grammar, based on this assumption, was incapable of generating certain sentences of English. The second of Chomsky's "three models for the description of language," phrase structure grammar, is much more satisfactory from this point of view. Any set of sentences that can be generated by a finite-state grammar can be generated by a phrase structure grammar. But the converse does not hold: there are sets of sentences that can be generated by a phrase structure grammar, but not by a finite-state grammar. This was one of the theorems that Chomsky proved in the more technical work that preceded the publication of *Syntactic Structures*. Let us express the relationship between phrase structure grammars and finite-state grammars by saying that phrase structure grammars are intrinsically more *powerful* than finite-state grammars (they can do everything that finite-state grammars can do—and more).

Consider the following English sentence (I have here taken one of Chomsky's own examples): *The man hit the ball.* It is made up of five words arranged in a particular order. We shall refer to the words out of which the sentence is composed as its *ultimate constituents* (implying that these elements are not further analyzable at the syntactic level). The order in which the ultimate constituents occur relative to one another may be described as the *linear structure* of the sentence. Now, linguists have generally claimed that sentences have another kind of syntactic structure in addition to, or independent of, their linear structure. A traditionally minded grammarian might say, of our simple model sentence, that (like all simple sentences) it has a *subject* and a *predicate*; that the subject is a *noun phrase* (*NP*), which consists of the *definite article* (*T*) and a *noun* (*N*); and that the predicate is a *verb phrase* (*VP*), which consists of a *verb* (*V*) with its *object*, which, like the subject, is a noun phrase consisting of the definite article and a noun. Essentially the same kind of description would have been given by "Bloomfieldian" linguists in terms of the notions of *immediate constituent analysis*: that the "immediate constituents" of the sentence (the two phrases into which it can be analyzed at the first stage) are the noun phrase *the man* (which has the role, or *function*, of subject), and the verb phrase *hit the ball* (which has the function of predicate); that the immediate constituents of *the man* are the article *the* and the noun *man*; that the immediate constituents of *hit the ball* are the verb *hit* and the noun phrase *the ball* (which has the function of object); and that the immediate constituents of *the ball* are the article *the* and the noun *ball*.

The notion of constituent structure, or *phrase structure* (to use Chomsky's term), is comparable to the notion of "bracketing" in mathematics or symbolic logic. If we have an expression of the form $x \times (y + z)$, we know that the operation of addition must be carried out first and the operation of multiplication afterward. By contrast, $x \times y + z$ is interpreted (by means of the general convention that, in the absence of brackets, multiplication takes precedence over addition) as being equivalent to $(x \times y) + z$. Generally speaking, the order in which the operations are carried out will make a difference to the result. For instance, with $x = 2, y = 3$, and $z = 5$: $x \times (y + z) = 16$, whereas $(x \times y) + z = 11$. There are many words in English and other languages that are ambiguous in much the same way that $x \times y + z$ would be ambiguous if it were not for the prior adoption by mathematicians of the general convention that multiplication takes precedence over addition. A classic example is the phrase *old men and women* (and more generally *A N and N*), which may be interpreted either as *(old men) and women*—cf., $(xy) + z$; or *old (men and women)*—cf., $x(y + z)$. Under the first interpretation the adjective *old* applies only to *men*;

under the second interpretation it applies both to *men* and to *women*. With the phrase structure indicated, by means of brackets, as *old {men and women}* the string of words we are discussing is semantically equivalent to (*old men*) *and* (*old women*)—cf., $x(y + z) = (xy) + (xz)$. We shall not pursue the mathematical analogy beyond this point. For our present purpose, it is sufficient to note that two strings of elements may have the same linear structure, but differ with respect to their phrase structure; and that the difference in their phrase structure may be semantically relevant.

The theoretical importance of this phenomenon, which we may refer to as *structural ambiguity* (Chomsky's term in *Syntactic Structures* is "constructional homonymity"), lies in the fact that the ambiguity of such strings as *old men and women* cannot be accounted for by appealing to a difference in the meaning of any of the ultimate constituents or to a difference of linear structure.

The theory of immediate constituent analysis had been much discussed by Chomsky's predecessors. Chomsky's major contribution with respect to this model of syntactic structure was first of all to show how it could be formalized by means of a system of generative rules and then to demonstrate that, although phrase structure grammar was more powerful and more satisfactory for the description of natural languages than finite-state grammar, it had certain limitations. Chomsky's formalization of phrase structure grammar may be illustrated by means of the following rules (which, with minor modifications, are identical with those given in *Syntactic Structures*):

(1) *Sentence* → *NP* + *VP*
(2) *NP* → *T* + *N*
(3) *VP* → *Verb* + *NP*
(4) *T* → *the*
(5) *N* → {*man, ball, ...*}
(6) *Verb* → {*hit, took, ...*}

This set of rules (which will generate only a small fraction of the sentences of English) is a simple phrase structure grammar.

Each of these rules is of the form $X → Y$, where X is a single element and Y is a *string* consisting of one or more elements. The arrow is to be interpreted as an instruction to replace the element that occurs to its left with the string of elements that occur to its right ("rewrite X as Y). Rules 5 and 6 employ brace brackets to list a set of elements any one of which, but only one of which, may be selected. (In each case only two members of the set have been given: the dots can be read as "etc.".) The rules are to be applied as follows. We start with the element *Sentence* and apply Rule 1: this yields the *string* (i.e., sequence of symbols: "string" is a technical term) $NP + VP$. We inspect this string to see whether any of the elements occurring in it can be rewritten by means of Rules 1–6. It will be seen that either Rule 2 or Rule 3 can be applied at this point: it does not matter which we select. Applying Rule 3, we get the string $NP + Verb + NP$. We can now apply Rule 2 twice, followed by Rules 4 and 5 twice, and Rule 6 once (in any order except that Rule 2 must precede Rules 4 and 5, as Rule 3 must precede Rule 6 and one of the applications of Rule 2). The *terminal string* generated by the rules (assuming that *man, hit,* and *ball* are selected at the appropriate points) is *the + man + hit + the + ball*; and it takes nine steps to generate this string of words. The set of nine strings, including the initial string, the terminal string, and seven intermediary strings constitute a *derivation* of the sentence *The man hit the ball* in terms of this particular phrase structure grammar. (The reader may wish to check his understanding of the rules by constructing a sample derivation himself.)

But how does this system assign to sentences the appropriate phrase structure? The answer to this question is given by a convention associated with the operation of "rewriting." Whenever we apply a rule we put brackets, as it were, around the string of elements that is introduced by the rule, and we label the string within the brackets as an instance of the element that has been rewritten by the rule. For example, the string *NP + VP* derived by Rule 1 is bracketed and labeled as *Sentence* (*NP + VP*). The labeled bracketing assigned to *NP + Verb + NP* is *Sentence* (*NP + VP* (*Verb + NP*)); and so on. An alternative, and equivalent, means of representing the labeled bracketing assigned to strings of elements generated by a phrase structure grammar is a *tree diagram*, as illustrated for our model sentence in Figure 2. Since tree diagrams are visually clearer than sequences of symbols and brackets, they are more commonly used in the literature, and we shall employ them (except for very simple instances) in what follows. The labeled bracketing, associated with a terminal string generated by a phrase structure grammar, is called a *phrase marker*.

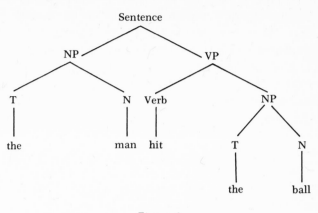

Figure 2

It will be obvious that the phrase marker given in Figure 2 conveys directly the following information: the string of terminal elements *the* + *man* + *hit* + *the* + *ball* is a *Sentence* that consists of two constituents, NP (*the man*) and VP (*hit the ball*); the NP, which occurs to the left of VP, consists of two constituents, T (*the*) and N (*man*); VP consists of two constituents, Verb (*hit*) and NP (*the ball*); and the NP that occurs to the right of *Verb* consists of two constituents, T (*the*) and N (*ball*). It thus represents all that we said earlier might have been considered relevant in an immediate constituent analysis of the sentence, except for the fact that *the man* is the subject, *hit the ball* is the predicate, and *the ball* is the object. But these notions, and in particular the distinction between the subject and the object, can also be defined in terms of the associated phrase

NOAM CHOMSKY | 66

marker.[1] The *subject* is that *NP* which is directly dominated by *Sentence* and the object is that *NP* which is
directly dominated by *VP*. What is meant by "domina-
tion" should be clear, without formal definition, from
the tree diagram. We shall need to appeal to this notion
in our discussion of transformational grammar in the
following chapter.

There are all sorts of different ways in which the small
phrase structure grammar with which we started out
could be extended and thus made capable of generating more and more sentences of English. The question is whether a grammar of this general type is, in
principle, adequate for the description of all the sentences that we should wish to regard as well formed,
or grammatical. Chomsky has not been able to prove
that there are sentences of English that cannot be generated by a phrase structure grammar (although it has
now been demonstrated that there do exist certain constructions in other languages, if not in English, that are
beyond the scope of phrase structure grammar in this
sense). What Chomsky claims, in *Syntactic Structures*
and elsewhere, is that there are sentences of English
which can be described only "clumsily" within the framework of phrase structure grammar—that is to say, in a
way that is "extremely complex, *ad hoc*, and 'unre-
vealing.'"

The important point to note is that Chomsky here
allows for the possibility that, although two grammars
may be equivalent in the sense that they each generate

---

[1] As Chomsky suggests in *Syntactic Structures*, p. 30, and
makes explicit later, notably in *Aspects of the Theory of
Syntax*, p. 71.

the same set of sentences (we shall refer to this as *weak equivalence*), there may yet be good reasons for considering one grammar to be preferable to the other. In *Syntactic Structures*, Chomsky claims that one of the main reasons for preferring a transformational grammar to a phrase structure grammar is that the former is, in a certain sense, simpler than the latter. It has proved very difficult, however, to make formally precise the sense in which the term "simplicity" is being employed here. How do we decide, for example, that a grammar that requires relatively few rules, some of which, however, are quite complex, for the generation of a given set of sentences is, as a whole, more or less "simple" than a second, weakly equivalent, grammar that requires far more rules, none of which, however, is particularly complex, to generate the same set of sentences? There is no obvious way of balancing one kind of simplicity against another.

In his later publications Chomsky attaches far less importance to the notion of "simplicity," and gives correspondingly more weight to the argument that transformational grammar reflects better the "intuitions" of the native speaker and is semantically more "revealing" than phrase structure grammar.[2] We can illustrate the defici-

---

[2] Chomsky tells me that he is not himself aware of any change in his attitude over the years with respect to the role of simplicity measures and intuition. He thinks that some confusion may have been caused by the fact that *Syntactic Structures* was "a rather watered-down version of earlier work (at that time unpublishable)" and that, for this reason, it "emphasized weak rather than strong generative capacity." I am sure that most linguists who read *Syntactic Structures* when it was first published in 1957 interpreted Chomsky's general views on linguistic theory in the way that I have

encies of phrase structure grammar from this point of view with reference to the generation of corresponding active and passive sentences in English: e.g., *The man hit the ball* and *The ball was hit by the man*. We have already seen how active sentences might be generated in a phrase structure grammar, and we could easily add further rules to the system in order to generate passive sentences. What we cannot represent within the framework of a phrase structure grammar, however, is the fact (and let us grant that it is a fact) that pairs of sentences like *The man hit the ball* and *The ball was hit by the man* are "felt" by native speakers to be related, or to "belong" together in some way, and to have the same or a very similar meaning. As we shall see in the following chapter, this relationship between corresponding active and passive sentences, as well as many other "intuitive" and semantic relationships, *can* be accounted for in a transformational grammar.

All the phrase structure rules introduced in this chapter so far have been *context-free*: that is to say, they have all been of the form $X \rightarrow Y$, where X is a single element and Y is a string of one or more elements, no reference being made to the context in which X is to be rewritten as Y. Consider, by contrast, a rule of the following form: $X \rightarrow Y/W - V$ (to be read as "X is to be rewritten as Y in the context of W to the left and V to the right"—there are various ways in which the contextual restrictions may be indicated). It is by means

___

represented them in Chapter IV. One can only wonder whether Chomsky's work would have had the effect that it did have within linguistics if *Syntactic Structures* had not been "watered down."

of a *context-sensitive* rule, cast in this form, that we might wish to account for the "agreement," or concord, that holds between the subject and the verb in English sentences (cf., *The boy runs*, but *The boys run*) and for similar phenomena in other languages; and we shall make use of context-sensitive rules in the next chapter. Here we may simply note that, from the formal point of view, context-free grammars can be regarded as a special subclass of context-sensitive grammars, this subclass being defined by the property that in each of the rules $X \rightarrow Y/W - V$ the contextual variables W and V are left "empty." It may be added that any set of sentences that can be generated by a context-free grammar can be generated by a context-sensitive grammar; the converse, however, is not true.

The statement that has just been made, which implies that context-sensitive grammars are intrinsically more powerful than context-free grammars (as context-free phrase structure grammars are intrinsically more powerful than finite-state grammars), illustrates again a very important, but highly technical, aspect of Chomsky's work, which we can do no more than mention in a book of this kind. The study of the formal properties and generative capacity of various types of grammar exists as a branch of mathematics or logic, independently of its relevance for the description of natural languages. The revolutionary step that Chomsky has taken, as far as linguistics is concerned, has been to draw upon this branch of mathematics (finite automata theory and recursive function theory) and to apply it to natural languages, like English, rather than to the artificial languages constructed by logicians and computer scientists. But he has done more than simply take over and adapt for the use of linguists an existing system of formalization and a set of theorems proved by others. He has made an independent and original contribution to the study of formal systems from a purely mathematical point of view. The mathematical investigation of phrase structure grammars, and more particularly of context-free phrase structure grammar, is now well advanced; and various degrees of equivalence have been proved between phrase structure grammar and other kinds of grammar, which also formalize the notion of "bracketing," or immediate constituent structure. So far the mathematical investigation of transformational grammar, which was initiated by Chomsky, has made relatively little progress. But transformational grammar, as we shall see in the next chapter, is a far more complex system than phrase structure grammar (although it may well be the case, as Chomsky claimed in *Syntactic Structures*, that it yields a "simpler" description of certain sentences).

Transformational Grammar

vii

We shall not go into a great deal of detail in our discussion of transformational grammar. However, it is impossible to understand Chomsky's more general views on the philosophy of language and mind unless one has some knowledge of the principal characteristics of the system of grammatical description that he founded some fifteen years ago and that has been under more or less continuous development since that time.

The first point that must be made is terminological. Whereas a phrase structure grammar is one that consists solely of phrase structure rules, a transformational grammar (as originally conceived by Chomsky) does not consist only of transformational rules. It includes a set of phrase structure rules as well. The transformational rules depend upon the previous application of the phrase structure rules and have the effect, not only of converting one string of elements into another, but, in principle, of changing the associated phrase marker. Furthermore, they are formally more heterogeneous and more complex than phrase structure rules. We give some examples of transformational rules presently. But we first need to introduce an appropriate set of phrase structure rules.

We will use those given by Chomsky[1]—with one or two minor changes:

(1) *Sentence* → *NP* + *VP*

(2) *VP* → *Verb* + *NP*

(3)
$$NP \rightarrow \begin{Bmatrix} NP_{sing} \\ NP_{pl} \end{Bmatrix}$$

(4) NP_{sing} → *T* + *N*

(5) NP_{pl} → *T* + *N* + *s*

(6) *T* → *the*

(7) *N* → {*man, ball, door, dog, book,* ...}

(8) *Verb* → *Aux* + *V*

(9) *V* → {*hit, take, bite, eat, walk, open,* ...}

(10) *Aux* → *Tense* (+ *M*) (+ *have* + *en*) (+ *be* + *ing*)

(11) *Tense* →
$$\begin{Bmatrix} Present \\ Past \end{Bmatrix}$$

(12) *M* → {*will, can, may, shall, must*}

---

[1] *Syntactic Structures*, p. 111.

It will be observed that this set of rules allows for a wider range of choices than those given in the previous chapter. Both singular and plural noun phrases are accounted for, by Rule 3; and a large number of tenses and moods are introduced (instead of just the simple past tense of *The man hit the ball*) by means of the element *Aux* and its subsequent development. Rule 10 implies that every string generated by it must contain the element *Tense* and may contain, in addition, one or more of the other strings of elements in brackets. (Elements like *s* in Rule 5 and *en* or *ing* in Rule 10 are morphemes rather than words. In fact, *have, be, the*, and all the elements listed on the right-hand side of Rules 7, 9, and 12 may also be regarded as morphemes. But we need not dwell here upon the difference between a "word" and a "morpheme" in linguistic theory.)

Assuming that the lists given in Rules 7 and 9 are considerably extended, this system of phrase-structure rules will generate a large (but finite) number of what we may call *underlying strings*. It should be emphasized that an underlying string (as indeed will be evident from the above rules) is not a sentence. The transformational rules have yet to be applied. One of the strings generated by these rules is *the + man + Present + may + have + en + open + the + door* (which, given the transformational rules of *Syntactic Structures*, underlies both the active sentence *The man may have opened the door* and the corresponding passive *The door may have been opened by the man*). The reader may wish to verify that this string is indeed generated by the rules and to construct the associated phrase marker.

Chomsky derived passive sentences from underlying strings in *Syntactic Structures* by means of an optional rule, which we may give, rather informally, as follows:

(13) $NP_1 + Aux + V + NP_2 \rightarrow NP_2 + Aux + be + en + V + by + NP_1$.

This rule differs in various respects from the phrase structure rules. Not just one element, but a string of four elements, appears to the left of the arrow; and the operation that is carried out by the rule is quite complex—involving the permutation of the two *NP*s (this is indicated by the subscripts) and the insertion of the elements *be, en,* and *by* at particular points.

There is, however, an even more important difference between the phrase structure rules (1–12) and the transformational rule (13); and this has to do with the way in which we interpret the symbols that occur in the rules. In a phrase structure rule a single symbol designates one and only one element in the string to which the rule applies. But in a transformational rule a single symbol may refer to a string of more than one element, provided that the string in question is *dominated* by (i.e., "derived from": see pp. 65-66) this symbol in the associated phrase marker. It is in this sense that transformational rules are said to operate upon phrase markers rather than simply upon strings of elements.

We shall first of all illustrate what is meant by this statement with reference to a purely abstract example. Given that the string $a + d + e + b + f + c + g + h$ has been generated by a set of phrase structure rules which assign to it the phrase marker illustrated in Figure 3 (the reader can easily reconstruct these rules for himself), this string will be converted by means of the transformational rule $B + D + E \rightarrow E + B$ into the string $c + g + h + a + d + e$ with the associated phrase marker shown in Figure 4. In other words, since the string of terminal symbols itself constitutes part of the phrase marker, we can say that the rule converts one phrase marker into another; and this is the defining property of transformational rules. The rule we have just given has the effect of deleting everything dominated by D (including D itself) and permuting B and E, keeping their internal structure intact. The phrase marker given in Figure 3 and the phrase marker given in Figure 4 may be described, respectively, as *underlying* and *derived*, with respect to the transformation in question. (In deciding that the derived phrase marker has the particular form I have attributed to it in Figure 4, I have begged an important theoretical question, to which we will return briefly in a moment.)

If we now look at our illustrative underlying string (*the + man + Present + may + have + en + open + the + door*) and at the associated phrase marker (which I have left the reader to construct for himself), we shall see that *the + man* is wholly dominated by NP, *Present + may + have + en* by Aux, V by V (this is an instance of "self-domination") and *the + door* by NP. This means that transformational Rule 13 is applicable and, if applied (for it is an optional rule), will convert the underlying string into Rule 13a with the appropriate derived phrase marker:

(13a) *the + door + Present + may + have + en + be + en + open + by + the + man*

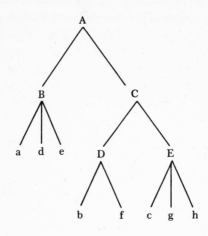

Figure 3

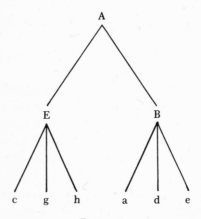

Figure 4

But what is the appropriate derived phrase marker? This is a difficult question. Granted that NP_2 becomes the subject of the passive sentence, that *be* + *en* becomes part of *Aux* in the same way that *have* + *en* or *may* is (this, as we shall see, is necessary for the operation of subsequent rules), and that *by* is attached to NP_1 to form a phrase, there are still a number of points about the structure of the derived phrase marker that remain unclear. Two possible phrase markers are given in Figures 5 and 6. It will be observed that they differ in that one takes *by* + NP_1 to be a part of the verb phrase, whereas the other treats it as an immediate constituent of the sentence, equivalent in "status," as it were, to NP_2 and *VP*. (It will also be noticed that I have put a question mark where the label for the bracketed phrase *by* + NP_1 should be.)

We have touched here on an important theoretical problem. The derived string produced by one transformational rule may serve as the underlying string for the operation of a subsequent transformational rule, and will therefore need to have associated with it the appropriate derived phrase marker. Chomsky and his followers have worked on this problem and have tried to establish a set of conventions according to which a particular kind of formal operation (e.g., deletion, permutation, or substitution) is defined to have a particular effect upon the topology of the phrase marker it transforms; and we followed these conventions when we decided that the effect of the rule $B + D + E \rightarrow E + B$, operating upon the underlying phrase marker shown in Figure 3, was the derived phrase marker in Figure 4. But this was a

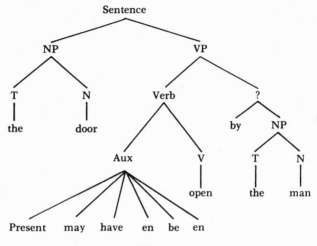

Figure 5

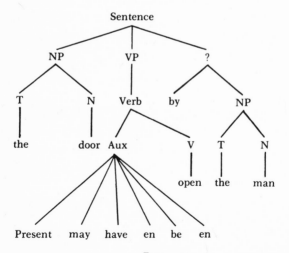

Figure 6

very simple example from the point of view of the operations involved and the shape of the phrase marker to which they applied; and furthermore it was a purely abstract example unaffected by any empirical considerations. The reader will appreciate that the situation is very different when it comes to formulating a set of transformational rules for the description of English or some other natural language.

We shall now introduce, and briefly discuss, two further transformational rules (slightly different in form from the corresponding rules in *Syntactic Structures*, but based upon them and having the same general effect). The first is the obligatory "number transformation":

$$(14) \quad Present \rightarrow \begin{cases} s \ / \ NP_{sing} \rule{2em}{0.4pt} \\ \emptyset \ / \ \text{elsewhere} \end{cases}$$

This is a context-sensitive rule, which says that *Present* is to be rewritten as *s* if and only if it is immediately preceded in the underlying string by a sequence of one or more elements dominated by NP_{sing} in the associated phrase marker, but is to be rewritten in all other contexts as "zero" (i.e., as the absence of a suffix). It is this rule which accounts for the "agreement" between subject and verb manifest in such sentences as *The man goes* vs. **The man go*, or *The man is . . .* vs. **The man are . . . .* If it is applied to Rule 13a it yields:

(14a) *the + door + s + may + have + en + be + en + open + by + the + man*

NOAM CHOMSKY | 80

It will be observed that what we might call the "abstract" verbal suffix *s* is here introduced *in front of* the element to which it is subsequently attached (in the same way that *en* and *ing* are introduced by phrase structure Rule 10 in front of the element to which they are later attached). We have called these "abstract" suffixes because, as we shall see, they assume a variety of forms, including "zero," in various contexts.

The rule by which these "abstract" suffixes are placed after the appropriate stems (the "auxiliary transformation") may be given as follows:

$$(15) \quad \left\{ \begin{array}{l} Tense \\ en \\ ing \end{array} \right\} + \left\{ \begin{array}{l} M \\ have \\ be \\ V \end{array} \right\} \rightarrow \left\{ \begin{array}{l} M \\ have \\ be \\ V \end{array} \right\} + \left\{ \begin{array}{l} Tense \\ en \\ ing \end{array} \right\}$$

This rule says that any pair of elements the first of which is *Tense*, *en*, or *ing*, and the second of which is *M*, *have*, *be*, or *V*, are to be (obligatorily) permuted, the rest of the string to the left and the rest of the string to the right remaining unchanged. If the rule is applied to 14a it will permute *s* + *may* (i.e., *Tense* + *M*), *en* + *be* and *en* + *open* (*en* + *V*), successively from left to right, yielding:

(15a) *the* + *door* + *may* + *s* + *have* + *be* + *en* + *open* + *en* + *by* + *the* + *man*

One more transformational rule has yet to apply, which puts a word-boundary symbol (we shall use a space) between every pair of elements the first of which is not *M, have, be,* or *V,* and the second of which is not *Tense, en,* or *ing.* Applied to Rule 15a, this yields:

(16a) *the door may + s have be + en open + en by the man*

And this is the form that our illustrative string would have after all the relevant transformational rules have operated.

Finally, in a grammar of the kind outlined by Chomsky in *Syntactic Structures,* there is a set of "morphophonemic" rules, which will convert the string of words and morphemes into a string of phonemes. These would rewrite *may + s* as the phonemic representation of what is spelled *may; open + en* as what is spelled *opened;* (*be + s* as what is spelled *is; run + en* as what is spelled *run;* and so on). We end up, therefore, as we should, with the phonemic representation of *The door may have been opened by the man.*

Those readers who were previously unfamiliar with Chomsky's system of transformational grammar may have found it rather tedious working through this step-by-step derivation of a single sentence. But they will now have acquired a sufficient understanding of the way the grammar is designed and operates for them to appreciate the significance of some of the more general points made in this and later chapters. At this stage in our discussion of transformational grammar, it may be helpful to introduce a diagram showing how the grammar outlined in *Syntactic Structures* was organized (see Figure 7). The input to the grammar is the initial ele-

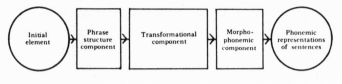

Figure 7

ment (as explained in the previous chapter), which generates a set of underlying strings by means of the phrase
structure rules in the first "box" of the diagram. The
second "box" comprises the transformational rules, of
which some are optional and others obligatory. These
rules take as their "input" single underlying strings, or
pairs of underlying strings (we shall come back to this
point), and by successively modifying these strings and
their associated phrase markers, generate as their "output" all and only the sentences of the language, represented as strings of words and morphemes, and assign
to each sentence its derived constituent structure. The
third "box" of rules then converts each of these sentences
from their syntactic representation as a string of words
and morphemes to their phonological representation as a
string of phonemes (and in this way relates the two
levels of analysis that were referred to in Chapter II under
the term "duality" of structure).

According to this model of generative grammar, different types of simple sentences are accounted for by
means of *optional* transformational rules. For example,
all the following sentences are related in that they derive
from the same underlying string:

(1) *The man opened the door.*

(2) *The man did not open the door.*

(3) *Did the man open the door?*

(4) *Didn't the man open the door?*

(5) *The door was opened by the man.*

(6) *The door was not opened by the man.*

(7) *Was the door opened by the man?*

(8) *Wasn't the door opened by the man?*

They differ in that: (1) has had no optional transformation applied to the underlying string; (2) has had the *Negative* transformation applied; (3) the *Interrogative*; (4) the *Negative* and *Interrogative*; (5) the *Passive*; (6) the *Passive* and *Negative*; (7) the *Passive* and *Interrogative*; and (8) the *Passive, Negative,* and *Interrogative*. Of these eight sentences, the first (a simple, active, declarative sentence) is defined by Chomsky, in *Syntactic Structures*, as a *kernel sentence*. It should be emphasized (and this is clear from our detailed consideration of the derivative of a passive sentence above) that non-kernel sentences, such as (2) (8), are not derived from kernel sentences, such as (1), but from a common underlying string. That is to say, there are no sentences generated without the application of at least a small number of *obligatory* transformations, including rules comparable in effect with Rules 14 and 15 above.

Compound sentences, in which two clauses are *co-ordinated* (e.g., *The man opened the door and switched on the light*), and complex sentences, in which one clause is *subordinated* to another (e.g., *The man who opened the door switched on the light*), are generated by means of *conjoining* and *embedding* transformations, respectively, which take as "input" a pair of underlying strings (e.g., *the + man + Past + open + the + door +* and *the + man + Past + switch + on + the + light*) and combine them in various ways. Conjoining and embedding transformations constitute the class of *generalized* transformations in *Syntactic Structures*; and it is the repeated application of these rules which accounts for the existence of such recursive structures as *This is the . . . that lived in the house that Jack built*, or *a big, black, three foot-long, . . . , wooden box* (see pp. 50-51). All the generalized transformations are of course optional.

So much, then, by way of a general summary of the earlier version of transformational grammar presented in *Syntactic Structures*. Chomsky claimed that one of the advantages of this system, the third and most powerful of his "models for the description of language," was that it could account more satisfactorily than phrase structure grammar for certain types of structural ambiguity. To take one of Chomsky's famous examples: a sentence like *Flying planes can be dangerous* is ambiguous (cf., *To fly planes can be dangerous* and *Planes which are flying can be dangerous*); and yet, under both interpretations, the immediate constituent analysis is, presumably, *(((flying) (planes)) (((can) (be)) (dangerous)))*. This is a different kind of structural ambiguity from that manifest in a phrase like *old men and women* discussed in the previous chapter. It would be possible to generate a sentence like *Flying planes can be dangerous* within a phrase structure grammar and to assign to it two different phrase markers—differing with respect to the labels assigned to the node dominating *flying*. But this would not be an intuitively satisfying account of the ambiguity; and it would fail to relate the phrase *flying planes*, on the one hand, to *planes which are flying*, and, on the other, to *someone flies planes*. The transformational analysis accounts for the ambiguity by relating two different underlying strings (let us say, *plane + s + be + ing + fly*, and *someone + fly + plane + s*) to the same derived string. Many other examples could be given of structurally ambiguous sentences that can be accounted for rather nicely in terms of transformational grammar: *I don't like eating apples* (i.e., "apples for eating" vs. "to eat apples"), *I disapprove of his drinking* (i.e., "the fact that he drinks" vs. "the way in which he drinks"; etc.[2]

This transformational explanation of structural ambiguity depends upon the application of *optional* rules; and it is in accord with the more general principle (which may be taken as axiomatic in the study of any system of communication) that meaning implies *choice*. This principle, it should be observed, states that the possibility of selecting one alternative rather than another is a *necessary*, but not a *sufficient*, condition for the expression of a difference of meaning. The most obvious application of the principle is when one word rather than another is selected from the set of words that could occur in a given position (cf., *The man opened the window* vs. *The man opened the door*). Here we are concerned with the "choice" of a different set of rules (or a difference in the order in which the same set of rules is applied) in the generation of two or more sentences from the same underlying string. I have said

[2] Cf. Chomsky, *Language and Mind*, p. 27.

that "choice," in this sense, is not a *sufficient* condition for there being a difference of meaning in the resultant sentences. For example, *John looked the word up in the dictionary* and *John looked up the word in the dictionary* differ (according to *Syntactic Structures*) in that an additional optional transformation has been applied in the generation of the former sentence. The two sentences are not, however, different in meaning; and the transformational rule in question (which has the effect of converting *Past + look + up + the + word* to *Past + look + the + word + up* at a particular point in the derivation) may be described as *stylistic*.

In 1965, in *Aspects of the Theory of Syntax*, Chomsky put forward a more comprehensive theory of transformational grammar, which differed from the earlier theory in a number of important respects. For our purpose, it will be sufficient to mention only the most general differences between the *Syntactic Structures* grammar and what we may call an *Aspects*-type grammar. Once again, a diagram may be helpful (see Figure 8).

The most striking difference between the two grammars, as represented in Figures 7 and 8, is the additional "box" of rules in the *Aspects*-type grammar labeled "Semantic Component." In *Syntactic Structures* it was argued that, although semantic considerations are not directly relevant to the syntactic description of sentences, there are "striking correspondences between the structures and elements that are discovered in formal, grammatical analysis and specific semantic functions," and that, "having determined the syntactic structure of the language, we can study the way in which this syntactic structure is put to use in the actual functioning

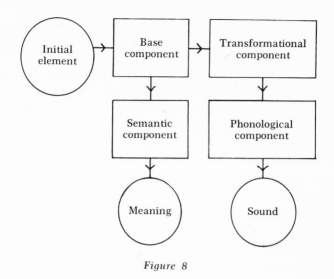

Figure 8

of the language."[3] In the years that followed the publication of *Syntactic Structures*, Chomsky and his collaborators came to the conclusion that the meaning of sentences could, and should, be submitted to the same kind of precise, formal analysis as their syntactic structure, and that semantics should be included as an integral part of the grammatical analysis of languages. The grammar of a language is now seen by Chomsky as a system of rules relating the meaning (or meanings) of each sentence it generates to the physical manifestation of the sentences in the medium of sound.

In *Aspects*, as in *Syntactic Structures*, the syntax falls into two parts. But the two syntactic components operate somewhat differently. It is now the *base* of the grammar

[3] *Syntactic Structures*, pp. 101, 102.

(which is roughly comparable with the phrase structure part of the earlier system), rather than the transformational component, that accounts for the semantically relevant options, including the possibility of forming recursive constructions. The difference between a declarative and an interrogative sentence, or between an active and a passive sentence, is no longer described in terms of optional transformations, but in terms of a choice made in the base rules. For example, there might be a base rule of the following form:

(2a) $VP \rightarrow Verb + NP\ (+ Agentive)$

and the selection of the element *Agentive* would distinguish the strings underlying passive sentences from the strings underlying the corresponding active sentences. There would then be an *obligatory* transformational rule, corresponding to Rule 13 (p. 74), operating if and only if the "input" string contained the element *Agentive*. This proposal (which corresponds with Chomsky's in spirit, rather than in detail) has the advantage that, if we formulate the transformational rule correctly, it gives us a label for the node dominating $by + NP_1$ in the derived phrase markers associated with passive sentences (p. 77).

The base rules generate an indefinitely large set of underlying phrase markers (which represent the *deep structure* of all the sentences characterized by the system); and these are converted into derived phrase markers (which represent the *surface structure* of the sentences) by the transformational rules, most of which (apart from "stylistic" rules) are now obligatory. The meaning of each sentence is derived, mainly if not wholly, from its deep structure, by means of the rules of semantic interpretation; and the phonetic interpretation of each sentence—its physical description as an acoustic "signal"—is derived from its surface structure by means of the phonological rules.

We need not go into the more technical details that distinguish an *Aspects*-type grammar from the conceptually simpler system of *Syntactic Structures.* All that remains to be added to this account of the general characteristics of the later version of transformational grammar is that various semantically relevant grammatical notions are now explicitly defined in terms of deep structure relations. (This was merely hinted at in *Syntactic Structures.*) We may note, in particular, the distinction between the "logical" (deep structure) and "grammatical" (surface structure) subject of a sentence. The "logical" subject is that *NP* which is immediately dominated by *S* (= *Sentence*) in the deep structure; the "grammatical" subject is the leftmost *NP* which is immediately dominated by (the topmost) *S* in the surface structure. For example, in the sentence *John was persuaded by Harry to take up golf*, the grammatical subject is *John* (it is this notion of "subject" which is relevant to the statement of the agreement holding between the subject and the verb in English: *John was persuaded* vs. *They were persuaded*, etc.). But the deep structure of this sentence consists of one sentence (S_2) embedded within another (S_1); and each sentence has its own logical subject. We can represent the deep structure of this sentence, informally and omitting all but the essential information, as it is given in Figure 9. It will be seen that the logical subject of S_1 (the *matrix* sentence)

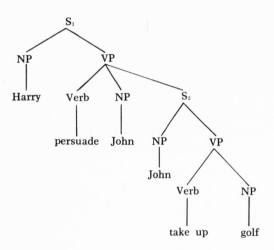

Figure 9

is *Harry*, and that of S_2 (the *embedded* sentence) is
John. Furthermore, the deep structure subject of S_2 is
identical with the deep structure object of S_1 (that *NP*
which is immediately dominated by *VP*). As Chomsky
points out, it is these deep structure relations that are
essential for the correct semantic interpretation of the
sentence.

The Psychological Implications
of Generative Grammar

● ● ●

VIII

As I emphasized in Chapter IV, the earlier works
of Chomsky were written within the tradition of
"autonomous" linguistics. It was only later, in
*Aspects of the Theory of Syntax, Cartesian Lin-
guistics,* and *Language and Mind,* that he began
to refer to linguistics as a branch of cognitive
psychology and to insist upon the importance of
generative grammar for the investigation of the
structure and predispositions of the human mind.
However, as I said in Chapter I, it is for these
later views, rather than for his more technical
contributions to linguistics as an independent
discipline, that Chomsky is now best known. We
shall therefore devote the next two chapters to
an exposition of Chomsky's current views on
these psychological and philosophical issues, di-
viding the material, somewhat arbitrarily as it

will appear, between the two headings of "psychology" and "philosophy."

Although Chomsky's general position in *Syntactic Structures* is, as far as he reveals it, indistinguishable from that of the "Bloomfieldians" and other empiricists, there is one point on which he has disagreed with Bloomfield and many of his followers from very early on. (I am not now referring to Chomsky's rejection of "discovery" in favor of "evaluation." This issue, which we discussed in a previous chapter, though important in the postwar development of linguistics, is in principle independent of the empiricist position.) Bloomfield, as we have seen, was a behaviorist (at the time that he wrote *Language*), and many of his followers shared his belief that a "mechanistic" account of language in terms of "stimulus-and-response" was more objective and more scientific than the traditional "mentalistic" description of language as a vehicle for the "expression of thought." In the year that *Syntactic Structures* was published, B. F. Skinner's *Verbal Behavior* also appeared; and it was reviewed in due course by Chomsky. Skinner (now retired from his position as Professor of Psychology at Harvard University) is one of the most eminent and most influential advocates of behaviorist psychology alive at the present time; and his book constitutes the most detailed attempt that has yet been made to account for the acquisition of language within the framework of behavioristic "learning theory." Chomsky's review is now a classic, in which he not only subjects Skinner's book to a penetrating examination, but at the same time reveals his own mastery of the relevant psychological literature.

Chomsky has since repeated his arguments against behaviorism on many occasions. Briefly, they amount to the following. One of the most striking facts about language is its "creativity"—the fact that by the age of five or six children are able to produce and understand an indefinitely large number of utterances that they have not previously encountered—and the behaviorist's "learning theory," however successful it might be in accounting for the way in which certain networks of "habits" and "associations" are built up in the "behavior-patterns" of animals and human beings, is totally incapable of explaining "creativity"—an aspect of human "behavior" manifest most clearly (though perhaps not exclusively) in language. Chomsky further claims that the terminology of behaviorism ("stimulus," "response," "habit," "conditioning," "reinforcement," etc.), though it can be made precise (and has been made precise in its application to more restricted domains), is so loose as actually applied to language, that it could cover anything and is thus completely devoid of empirical content. In the absence of any overt "response," the behaviorist takes refuge in an unobserved and unobservable "disposition to respond"; and having accounted, in principle, for the association of words (as "responses") with objects (as "stimuli") and for the learning of a limited set of sentences in the same way, he either says nothing at all about the formation of new sentences or at this point appeals to some undefined notion of "analogy."

Chomsky's criticisms of behaviorism are undoubtedly valid. It does not follow, of course (and as far as I know Chomsky has never claimed that it does), that no aspects of language, or the use of language, can be reasonably described in terms of a "stimulus-and-response" model. There can be little doubt, however, that the behaviorist account of the acquisition of language, as formulated at present, fails to come to grips with, let alone solve, the problem posed by what Chomsky calls "creativity."

Neither the earlier nor the later version of transformational grammar is presented by Chomsky as a psychological model of the way people construct and understand utterances. The grammar of a language, as conceived by Chomsky, is an idealized description of the linguistic *competence* of native speakers of that language (see p. 45). Any psychological model of the way this competence is put to use in actual *performance* will have to take into account a number of additional factors, which the linguist deliberately ignores in his definition of the notion of *grammaticality*. These psychologically relevant factors include the limitations of human memory and attention, the time it takes for neural "signals" to pass from the brain to the muscles that are involved in speech, the interference of one physiological or psychological process with another, and so on. Many of the sentences that the linguist regards as grammatical (well formed in terms of the rules set up to describe the competence of the "ideal" native speaker) would never in fact occur "naturally"; and, if constructed deliberately for the purpose of some linguistic experiment, will be difficult, and perhaps impossible, for actual native speakers to understand, because they cannot be "processed" without "overloading" the various psychological mechanisms involved in the reception and comprehension of speech. This is one way in which the utterances actually produced by speakers of a language might differ significantly, for psychologically explicable reasons, from the sentences described as "grammatical" by the linguist. Another difference, and one that Chomsky has more frequently stressed, is that the utterances produced will contain a variety of mistakes and distortions (mispronunciations, unfinished sentences, hesitations, changes of construction in the middle of a sentence, etc.) due to the malfunctioning of the psychological mechanisms involved or to their inherent limitations. These deviations from the grammatical norm are a valuable part of the psychologist's data and, when properly analyzed, may give him some insight into the structure and operation of the mechanisms underlying the use of language.

Although linguistics and psychology take a different point of view with respect to the investigation of language, Chomsky has always maintained that there are important connections between the two disciplines. In fact, the change that one can discern between his earlier and later view of the relationship between psychology and linguistics (to which I have already referred) is largely a matter of emphasis. If Chomsky now describes linguistics as a branch of psychology rather than as an independent discipline, he is not suggesting that the linguist should turn from the investigation of language to the investigation of the use of language, from linguistic competence to linguistic performance. What he is saying is that the most important reason for being interested in the scientific study of language, and more especially in generative grammar, is that it has a contribution to make to our understanding of mental processes. Linguistics is incorporated in psychology, therefore, not by virtue of any substantial change in subject matter or method, but for the ultimate significance of its results.

Even Chomsky's appeal to "intuition," which is more prominent in his later work (and which has frequently been misunderstood), can be interpreted in this light. According to Chomsky, two grammars may be *observationally* adequate (and weakly equivalent) in that they both generate the same set of sentences. But one will be *descriptively* more adequate than the other if it is in accord with the "intuitions" of native speakers, with respect to such questions as "structural ambiguity" and the equivalence or non-equivalence of certain types of sentences. This is the terminology used in *Aspects of the Theory of Syntax* and in other recent works. The terminological distinction is revealing. It shows that for Chomsky the "intuitions" of the speaker (that is to say, his mental representation of the grammar of the language), rather than the sentences themselves, are the true object of description. As we saw in Chapter IV, Chomsky had previously laid more stress on "simplicity" as a criterion for the evaluation of weakly equivalent grammars; and, when he did talk of the speaker's judgments with respect to such questions as "structural ambiguities," it was never suggested that these judgments, or "intuitions," were of primary concern: they testified to the informant's apprehension of the structure of his language, but they did not themselves constitute the subject matter of linguistics. It is sometimes thought that Chomsky's appeal to the "intuitions" of the native speaker (including the "intuitions" of the linguist as a speaker of his own native language) implies some re-

laxation of the standards of rigor and objectivity characteristic of "Bloomfieldian" linguistics and other modern
approaches. This is not so. Chomsky does not claim that
the speaker's "intuitions" are immediately accessible; nor
does he say that they are all equally reliable. It is arguable that some of the work inspired by Chomsky's formulation of the goals of linguistics rests on a too ready
acceptance of a particular linguist's "intuitions." In
principle, however, whether a given sentence is acceptable, whether it is equivalent to some other sentence or
not, and what its implications are—all these and similar
questions that fall within the scope of the native
speaker's "intuition," as Chomsky uses this term, are
subject to empirical verification.

As early as 1958 Chomsky collaborated with the psychologist George Miller in writing a paper entitled "Finite
State Languages," and in 1963 they contributed two
chapters to the *Handbook of Mathematical Psychology*
(there is also a further chapter written by Chomsky
alone). One of these chapters by Miller and Chomsky,
"Finitary Models of Language Users," draws in some
detail the implications of generative grammar for the
investigation of the psychological mechanisms underlying linguistic performance.

It follows immediately from Chomsky's proof that
finite-state grammars are incapable of generating some
of the sentences to be found in English and other languages, that no performance model based on the same
principle of "left-to-right" derivation is worthy of serious
consideration. We can therefore exclude all those theories of the production and reception of speech which
assume that the probability of occurrence of a given word

in a particular position in an utterance is determined solely by the words that have been selected for the preceding positions. It may not seem very plausible that anyone should seek to account for the production of an utterance such as *We have just been running* by saying that the speaker first selects *we* from the set of words permissible at the beginning of English sentences and then, having made this choice, selects *have*, as one of the words that has a certain probability of occurrence after *we*; then, having chosen *we* and *have*, selects *just*, by virtue of its probability of occurrence after *we have*; and so on. Plausible or not (and common-sense "plausibility" is after all not always reliable), this conception of the production of the speech has inspired a considerable amount of psychological research (including, it might be added, some of George Miller's earlier work). Chomsky has proved that this approach is misguided, despite the sophistication of the statistical theory it draws upon.

The second of Chomsky's "models for the description of language" was phrase structure grammar; and, as we saw in Chapter VI, various kinds of phrase structure grammars can be constructed according to the restrictions imposed upon the format or mode of operation of the rules. It is an interesting fact, as proved by Chomsky, that context-free phrase structure grammars are equivalent in generative capacity to what are called *pushdown storage* devices in *automata theory*. We cannot go into this highly technical question in any detail, but it may be mentioned briefly, in order to give the reader some idea of the kind of hypotheses about performance models that can be suggested by a study of the formal properties of language and the generative capacity of particular types of grammar.

The human memory, as we have said, has presumably only a finite (though perhaps very large) amount of storage at its disposal, and it may operate, to some extent at least, on the "push-down" principle of "last in, first out," so that, other things being equal, we recall most easily and most quickly what we have "stored" in memory most recently. It is reasonable to suppose that the *long-term*, or permanent, memory contains a good deal of information, including the rules of the grammar, to which access is made during the "processing" of utterances. But we are concerned here with what psychologists call the *short-term* memory, which we use, for example, when we commit to memory (without learning or repetition) a list of unconnected items (e.g., nonsense syllables or digits). There are very severe limits upon the capacity of short-term memory, the number of items that we can "store" there being of the order of seven ("seven plus or minus two," as Miller put it in the title of a famous paper). So much is background information relevant to the hypothesis we are about to discuss.

This is the so-called "depth hypothesis," developed about ten years ago by Victor Yngve, who was at that time working on the problems of syntactic analysis by computer. Let us begin by giving a purely abstract example of a phrase structure grammar, which includes a number of recursive rules:

(1) $A \rightarrow B + C$ (6) $D \rightarrow \{d, \ldots\}$

(2) $B \rightarrow (B) + D$ (7) $E \rightarrow \{e, \ldots\}$

$(3)\ B \rightarrow E + (B)$ $(8)\ F \rightarrow \{f, \ldots\}$

$(4)\ B \rightarrow F + (B) + G$ $(9)\ G \rightarrow \{g, \ldots\}$

$(5)\ C \rightarrow \{c, \ldots\}$

(I have followed a common convention in using capitals for auxiliary elements and lower case letters for terminal elements.) It will be observed that Rules 2, 3, and 4 are recursive, but in different ways. Rule 2 is *left recursive*; Rule 3 is *right recursive*; and Rule 4 is *self-embedding*. Figures 10, 11, and 12 illustrate what is meant by these terms.

Now, Yngve's hypothesis was that left-recursive structures add to the "depth," or psychological complexity, of a sentence, because recursion to the left, unlike recursion to the right, increases the amount of "space" taken up in the short-term memory during the processing of the sentence. When the "depth" of a sentence goes beyond the critical limit (this limit being determined by the capacity of the short-term memory), its continuation becomes unmanageable. And one of the reasons why there are transformations in language, Yngve suggested, is to enable the speaker to avoid excessive "depth" by using equivalent right-branching constructions, rather than left-branching constructions, at certain points in the production of sentences. This hypothesis predicts, therefore, that a phrase like *John's friend's wife's father's gardener's daughter's cat* should be more difficult to "process" than the equivalent right-branching version, *The cat belonging to the daughter of the gardner of the father of the wife of the friend of John.*

The "depth hypothesis," as formulated by Yngve, is almost certainly incorrect, since it rests on the assump-

Figure 10

Figure 11

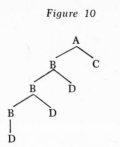

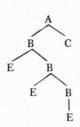

Figure 12

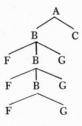

tion that sentences are "processed" by human beings in the way that they were generated by his computer program. Moreover, it is not clear that left-branching structures are as difficult for human beings to "process" as they should be according to the hypothesis. English has a variety both of left-recursive and right-recursive constructions; and there may well be a general tendency, as Yngve claimed, to avoid excessive "depth" by taking advantage of this fact. But there are other languages, including Turkish and Japanese, where the recursive constructions are predominantly left-branching.

Furthermore, as Chomsky has pointed out in his discussion of Yngve's hypothesis, it is *self-embedding* constructions (as exemplified in Figure 12) that seem to cause the greatest difficulty; and this cannot be explained in terms of the notion of "depth." As a simple example of self-embedding, consider a sentence like *The book the man left is on the table.* Here we have one sentence *The man left the book* (strictly speaking, the string underlying this sentence) embedded in the middle of *The book is on the table* (and subjected to a variety of other operations, including the deletion of *the book* in the embedded relative clause). The resultant complex sentence is perfectly acceptable. But let us now embed yet another sentence in the middle of the previously embedded clause: *The book the man the gardener saw left is on the table.* It is a moot point whether this sentence is acceptable or not. And if we embed a further sentence within *the gardener saw* (*the man*), to yield, let us say, *The book the man the gardener I employed yesterday saw left is on the table,* we will surely say that the "output" is unacceptable. Such sentences, despite the formal simplicity of the process of self-embedding, are undeniably difficult to "process" in both the production and the reception of speech. The explanation, as Chomsky says, cannot be simply that there are severe limitations on the capacity of the short-term memory (although this is no doubt one of the factors involved), because *self*-embedding constructions are significantly more difficult to "process" than other constructions derived by the embedding of one element in the middle, rather than at the left or right of a string. In other words, all structures generated by means of a rule of the form $X \rightarrow V + (Y) + W$ (where V and W are strings of one or more elements) involve the temporary "storage" of W while Y is being "processed." Self-embedding occurs when a rule has the more specific property that X and Y take the same "value" (as in Rule 4, p. 100). The identity of X and Y appears to introduce additional complexity from the point of view of production and comprehension. Chomsky and Miller have suggested, as a hypothesis capable in principle of explaining this fact, that the underlying psychological mechanism is of such a kind that it cannot, or can only with difficulty, execute a particular operation if it is already in the midst of executing the same operation.

It should be clear from this discussion of Yngve's "depth" hypothesis and Chomsky's hypothesis about self-embedding that the investigation of the formal properties of generative grammar can have suggestive implications for the study of the psychological "mechanisms" underlying linguistic performance. In conclusion, we shall refer briefly to a number of psychological experiments that have been inspired by transformational grammar.

As we saw in the previous chapter, the way in which Chomsky accounted for the relationship between corresponding active and passive sentences, corresponding affirmative and negative sentences, corresponding declarative and interrogative sentences, and so on, was by means of a set of optional transformational rules (one of which, the passive transformation, we have studied in some detail). Under this analysis, kernel sentences (simple, affirmative, active, declarative sentences, such as *John was reading a book*), were simpler in terms of the number of rules applied than non-kernel sentences. It was tempting to postulate that kernel sentences were not only linguistically simpler (i.e., in terms of a particular model of competence), but also psychologically simpler, and, assuming a close correspondence between competence and performance, to set up experiments designed to test the psychological validity of transformational processes.

The results of some of the earlier experiments were very encouraging. It was shown, for example, that active sentences could be remembered more easily than passive sentences, and affirmative sentences more easily than negative sentences. Even more strikingly, in an experiment based on the time taken to respond to different types of sentences, it was demonstrated, not only that the "latencies," or reaction times, were longer for passive sentences and negative sentences, but that the difference between the latency for corresponding affirmative active sentences and negative passive sentences was equal to the sum of the differences for affirmative active and affirmative passive sentences, on the one hand, and for affirmative active and negative active sentences, on the other. This could be interpreted as a confirmation of the hypothesis that the "processing" of sentences included a set of transformational operations, each of which took a certain fixed amount of time to carry out.

These experiments were, in fact, vitiated by a failure to take into account a number of relevant factors. However we describe the difference between active and passive sentences in English, it is quite clear that the greater "naturalness" of one rather than the other depends upon the kind of noun phrase or nouns that occur as the underlying subject and object, whether they are definite or indefinite, whether they refer to human beings or things, etc. For instance, *John was reading a book* is more "natural" than *A book was being read by John*; but the passive sentence *John was hit by a car* is more "natural" than the corresponding active sentence *A car hit John*. Unless the corresponding active and passive sentences in an experiment of the kind referred to above are equally "natural," one cannot be sure what is the source of the additional psychological complexity that is being measured by the differences in the latencies. A further potentially relevant factor is the difference in the length of corresponding active and passive sentences. Any experiment that is designed to test the psychological validity of a particular grammatical model must evidently control all the relevant, or potentially relevant, performance variables, as far as these can be determined. In the last few years psychologists whose research has been directly inspired by generative grammar seem to have become more aware of this problem.

The Philosophy of Language and Mind

●

IX

We now turn from the psychological to the more philosophical implications of generative grammar. It should be remembered, however, that this distinction I am drawing is, as I said at the beginning of the previous chapter, somewhat arbitrary. For it is part of Chomsky's case that linguistics, psychology, and philosophy are no longer to be regarded as separate and autonomous disciplines.

Chomsky believes that linguistics can make an important contribution to the study of the human mind and that, even now, it provides evidence in favor of one position rather than the other in the long-standing philosophical dispute between *rationalists* and *empiricists*. The difference between these two doctrines, at its most extreme, is as follows: the rationalist claims that the mind (or "reason"—hence the term "rationalism") is the sole source of human knowledge, the empiri-

cist that all knowledge derives from experience ("empiricism" comes from the Greek word for "experience"). But
there are, of course, less extreme formulations of the
difference; and in the long history of Western philosophy
the debate between representatives of the two camps has
taken a variety of forms.

In the seventeenth and eighteenth centuries, and in
a good deal of European and American philosophy since
then, one of the main points at issue has been the relationship between the mind (if there is such a thing, as
many empiricists would deny) and our perception of
the external world. Is this simply a matter of the passive
registration of sense-impressions and their subsequent
combination in terms of laws of "association," as the
British empiricists, Locke, Berkeley, and Hume, claimed
was the case? Or should we say, rather, with such philosophers as Descartes, that our perception and understanding of the external world rests upon a number of
"ideas" (that is, the knowledge of certain propositions
and certain principles of interpretation) and that these
"ideas" are "innate," and not derived from experience?
The empiricist doctrine has been very influential in the
development of modern psychology; and, combined with
physicalism and *determinism*, it has been responsible
for the view, held by many psychologists, that human
knowledge and human behavior are wholly determined
by the environment, there being no radical difference
in this respect between human beings and other animals,
or indeed between animals and machines. (By "physicalism" is meant, in this context, the philosophical system according to which all statements made about a
person's thoughts, emotions, and sensations can be re-

formulated as statements about his bodily condition and observable behavior, and can thus be brought within the scope of "physical" laws; by "determinism" is meant the doctrine that all physical events and phenomena, including those actions and decisions of human beings that we might describe as resulting from "choice" or "free will," are determined by earlier events and phenomena and are subject to the laws of cause-and-effect, so that our impression of freedom of choice is totally illusory. Behaviorism, to which reference was made in the discussion of Bloomfield's theory of language in Chapter III, is therefore a particular version of physicalism and determinism.) Chomsky's view of man is very different: he believes that we are endowed with a number of specific faculties (to which we give the name "mind") that play a crucial role in our acquisition of knowledge and enable us to act as free agents, undetermined (though not necessarily unaffected) by external stimuli in the environment. These are the issues that Chomsky deals with in many of his most recent publications, most notably in *Cartesian Linguistics* and *Language and Mind*. Before plunging into these deep and turbulent waters, it will be as well to discuss the linguistic evidence to which Chomsky appeals as a support for his rationalist philosophy.

As we have seen, "Bloomfieldian" linguistics was remarkably, and at times almost ostentatiously, uninterested in general theoretical questions. Most American linguists (and many linguists in other parts of the world too, it must be admitted), if they had been asked, ten or fifteen years ago, what was the main purpose of linguistics, would probably have said that it was "to describe languages"; and they might well have referred to the practical advantages of a training in the subject for anthropologists, missionaries, and others whose business it was to communicate with peoples speaking a language for which grammars had not yet been written. They would have left the matter at that. Very few of them, if any, would have given the kind of answer that Sapir had suggested to this question in his book *Language*, published a generation before: that language is worth studying because it is unique to man and indispensable for thought. Indeed, they might well have challenged the propriety of using the word "language" in the singular in the way that I have just done, since this tends to imply that all languages have something in common, and the "Bloomfieldians," as we have seen, were rather skeptical on this point. Bloomfield himself had said, in a much-quoted passage, that "the only useful generalizations about language are inductive generalizations," and that "features which we think ought to be universal may be absent from the very next language that becomes accessible."

Chomsky's attitude, as expressed in his most recent publications, is radically opposed to Bloomfield's. He holds that it is the central purpose of linguistics to construct a deductive theory of the structure of human language that is at once sufficiently general to apply to all languages (and not only all known languages, but also all possible languages—we will come back to this) and not so general that it would also be applicable to other systems of communication or anything else that we should not wish to call languages. In other words, linguistics should determine the universal and essential properties of human language. In fact, Chomsky's position on this point is similar, as he acknowledges, to that of the Russian linguist Roman Jakobson, who has been resident in the United States for a number of years and has long been one of the most outspoken critics of the "Bloomfieldian" tradition.

Like Jakobson, Chomsky believes that there are certain phonological, syntactic, and semantic units that are *universal*, not in the sense that they are necessarily present in all languages, but in the somewhat different, and perhaps less usual, sense of the term "universal," that they can be defined independently of their occurrence in any particular language and can be identified, when they do occur in particular languages, on the basis of their definition within the general theory. For example, it is held that there is a fixed set of up to twenty *distinctive features* of phonology (e.g., the feature of *voicing* that distinguishes *p* from *b* or *t* from *d* in the pronunciation of the English words *pin* and *bin* or *ten* and *den*, or the feature of *nasality* that distinguishes *b* from *m* or *d* from *n* in *bad* and *mad* or *pad* and *pan*). Not all of these will be found in the phonemes of all languages; but from their various possible combinations every language will, as it were, make its own selection. Similarly at the level of syntax and semantics. Such syntactic categories as Noun or Verb or Past Tense, and such components of the meaning of words as "male" or "physical object," belong to fixed sets of elements, in terms of which it is possible to describe the syntactic and semantic structure of all languages, although no particular language will necessarily manifest all the elements recognized as "universal" in the general theory.

These phonological, syntactic, and semantic elements are what Chomsky calls the *substantive universals* of linguistic theory.

Far more characteristic of Chomsky's thought, and more original, is his emphasis on what he refers to as *formal universals*; that is, the general principles that determine the form of the rules and the manner of their operation in the grammars of particular languages. For example, the transformations that relate various sentences and constructions, Chomsky claims, "are invariably *structure-dependent* in the sense that they apply to a string of words by virtue of the organization of these words into phrases."[1] All the transformations that we discussed in Chapter VII (and notably the passive transformation) satisfy this condition, since, as we saw, their applicability was determined by the analyzability of the "input" string with reference to the associated phrase marker (and this is what Chomsky means by "structure-dependency"). It is an important fact about language, says Chomsky, that it does not make use of structure-independent operations in order to relate one sentence type, let us say, to another. For example, the relationship between the declarative sentence *John was here yesterday* and the corresponding interrogative *Was John here yesterday?* might seem at first sight to be describable in terms of a simple operation permuting the first and second words (with an accompanying change of intonation, which we will neglect here). This operation would be structure-independent, if it were specified by means of a rule that made no reference to the syntactic function of *John* and *was*. Consideration of a wider class of

[1] *Language and Mind*, p. 51.

examples (such as *His elder brother was here yesterday* and *Was his elder brother here yesterday?*, *The blast-off took place on time* and *Did the blast-off take place on time?*) shows us that the rule must be expressed somewhat as follows (to put it informally): "Permute the whole of the subject noun phrase with the first auxiliary verb, introducing the auxiliary verb *do* for the purpose, when there is no other." It thus turns out that those sentences, like *John was here yesterday* and *Was John here yesterday?*, which can be related by means of a rule of the form "Permute the first two words," also fall within the scope of the more general structure-dependent rule: it just happens to be that the subject noun phrase is a single word and occupies the first position of the declarative sentence and the second word is an auxiliary verb. According to Chomsky, it will always prove to be the case that what appear to be valid structure-independent operations are special instances of more general structure-dependent operations.

Chomsky and his associates have tentatively proposed a number of more specific universal constraints upon the operation of grammatical rules. Limitations of space prevent us from mentioning more than one of these. We will take what Chomsky calls the "A-over-A" principle (which is one of the three constraints he discusses in *Language and Mind*). This means that, if a transformational rule makes reference to a phrase of type A and the string of elements to which the rule applies contains two such phrases, one being included within the other, the rule will operate only upon the larger phrase. (In the associated phrase marker the larger phrase of type A dominates the phrase of type A that it includes.) Obvious examples of strings of elements that come within the scope of this principle are noun phrases that contain noun phrases. For instance, *the book on the desk* is a noun phrase, and *the desk*, which is included within it, is also a noun phrase. According to the "A-over-A" principle, any rule that moves, deletes, or otherwise operates upon noun phrases could apply to the whole phrase *the book on the desk*, but not to *the desk*. There are a number of facts in the grammar of English and other languages that appear to be satisfactorily explained in terms of this general principle. On the other hand, as Chomsky points out, there are certain rules that violate the principle, although they appear to be otherwise well motivated; and in the present state of research it is not clear whether the "A-over-A" principle should just be abandoned or whether it is possible to modify it in such a way that it will cover the exceptions also. And this seems to hold for all the more specific constraints that have been proposed so far: they are only partially satisfactory, since they explain only some of the relevant data. Although the "A-over-A" principle, as it is at present formulated, is, by Chomsky's own admission, probably not valid, it will serve as an illustration of the kind of constraints upon the application of grammatical rules that Chomsky has in mind when he talks of the formal universals of linguistic theory.

It may be worth pointing out that, as far as substantive universals are concerned, Chomsky's view is not necessarily in conflict with Bloomfield's, since Chomsky accepts that any one of his allegedly universal features might be absent, not only "from the very next language that becomes accessible," but also from very many quite familiar languages. It is for this reason I referred earlier to the difference between Chomsky's view of "universals" and the "Bloomfieldian" view as one of "attitude." Bloomfield and his "structuralist" disciples, for reasons that were explained in Chapter III, followed Boas in stressing the diversity of human languages; Chomsky emphasizes their similarities. Clearly, one must give due recognition to the differences of grammatical structure that are found throughout the languages of the world. But there can be little doubt that the "Bloomfieldians," as well as many other schools of linguists, in their anxiety to avoid the bias of traditional grammar, have tended to exaggerate these differences and have given undue emphasis to the principle that every language is a law unto itself. The grammatical similarities that exist between widely separated and historically unrelated languages are at least as striking as their differences. Moreover, recent work in the syntactic analysis of a number of languages lends support to the view that the similarities are deeper and the differences more superficial.

Chomsky himself has been more cautious than some of his followers in accepting that languages are more similar in their deep structure than they are in their surface structure. He attaches far more importance to the fact (and let us grant, provisionally, that it is a fact) that different languages make use of the same formal operations in the construction of grammatical sentences. And it is upon this kind of similarity between languages, as we shall see presently, that he rests his case for a rationalist philosophy of language.

It will be recalled that finite state grammars and

phrase structure grammars were criticized by Chomsky as being insufficiently powerful for the description of natural languages. Paradoxical though it may appear at first sight, one of the most obvious deficiencies of current versions of transformational grammar, as Chomsky has pointed out, is that they are *too* powerful. There is an extremely important principle involved here; and it is essential to an understanding of Chomsky's notion of "universal grammar." When we discussed "the goals of linguistic theory" in Chapter IV, we saw that the linguist, in writing a generative grammar of a particular language, sets himself the task of characterizing "all and only" the sentences of that language. (This is of course an ideal, at present unrealized for any natural language: but this does not affect the principle.) The same point holds on the more general plane. Linguistic theory, as we have seen, should be both general enough to cover all particular languages, and yet not so general that it will apply to other systems of communication (and thereby define them implicitly as "languages"). Transformational grammar, in its present form, allows for the possibility of a variety of operations and various ways of building up sequences of operations which, as far as we know, are not required for the description of any human language. This means that it is more general than it need be as a theory of the structure of human language. The problem is to decide whether there are any formal limitations that we can incorporate in the theory of transformational grammar such that the grammars of particular languages written within these deliberately imposed limitations will not only be in principle capable of accounting for all the sentences that are actually found in those languages, but will exclude as *theoretically* impossible the maximum number of non-sentences. As we have seen, Chomsky believes that there are certain very specific conditions that govern the operation of grammatical rules in all languages; and it is by means of these conditions, provided that they can be determined and formalized, that he proposes to restrict the power of transformational grammar.

We now come to the philosophical consequences of Chomsky's notion of universal grammar. If all human languages are strikingly similar in structure, it is natural to ask why this should be so. It is equally natural, or so it might appear to an empiricist philosopher, to answer this question by appealing to such obviously relevant facts as the following: all human languages make reference to the properties and objects of the physical world, which, presumably, is perceived in essentially the same way by all physiologically and psychologically normal human beings; all languages, in whatever culture they might operate, are called upon to fulfill a similar range of functions (making statements, asking questions, issuing commands, etc.); all languages make use of the same physiological and psychological "apparatus," and the very way in which this operates may be held responsible for some of the formal properties of language. Now all these facts are, as I have said, relevant; and they may well have exerted an influence upon the structure of language. But many of the universal features of language, both substantive and formal, are not readily explained in this way. The only conceivable explanation, says Chomsky, in terms of our present knowledge at least, is that human beings are genetically endowed with a highly specific "language faculty" and that it is this "faculty" which determines such universal features as structure-dependency or the "A-over-A" principle (to take the two examples mentioned earlier in this chapter). It is at this point that Chomsky makes contact with the rationalist tradition in philosophy.

Chomsky's conclusion is reinforced, he claims, by a consideration of the process by which children learn their native language. All the evidence available suggests that children are not born with a predisposition to learn any one language rather than any other. We may therefore assume that all children, regardless of race and parentage, are born with the same ability for learning languages; and, in normal circumstances, children will grow up as what we call "native speakers" of that language which they hear spoken in the community in which they are born and spend their early years. But how does the child manage to develop that creative command of his native language which enables him to produce and understand sentences he has never heard before? Chomsky maintains that it is only by assuming that the child is born with a knowledge of the highly restrictive principles of universal grammar, and the predisposition to make use of them in analyzing the utterances he hears about him, that we can make any sense of the process of language learning. Empiricist theories of language learning cannot bridge the gap between the relatively small number of utterances (many of them full of errors, distortions, and hesitations) which the child hears about him and his ability to construct for himself on the basis of this scanty and imperfect data, in a relatively short time, the grammatical rules of the language. It is the child's inborn knowledge of the universal principles governing the structure of human language that supplies the deficiency in the empiricist account of language acquisition. These principles are part of what we call the "mind," being represented in some way, no doubt, in the structure or mode of operation of the brain, and may be compared with the "innate ideas" of Descartes and the rationalist tradition going back to Plato.

Chomsky's theory of transformational grammar was originally formulated, as I have stressed throughout this book, within the framework of "autonomous" linguistics. Such few references as there are in his earlier writings to philosophical issues would suggest that he, like most other linguists and psychologists, saw no reason to dispute the empiricist theory of knowledge and perception. This fact should be borne in mind in any assessment of his current philosophical views. Having been trained himself in the predominantly empiricist tradition of modern science, he is well aware that his notion of the genetic transmission of the principles of universal grammar will strike many philosophers and scientists as absurdly fanciful. As he pointed out in his radio discussion with Stuart Hampshire: "The empiricist view is so deep-seated in our way of looking at the human mind that it almost has the character of a superstition."[2] After all, we do not accuse the biologist of unscientific mysticism when he postulates the genetic transmission and subsequent maturation of the quite complex "instinctual" behavior patterns characteristic of various species. Why should we be so ready to believe that human behavior,

[2] Printed in *The Listener*, May 30, 1968.

which is demonstrably more complex and more flexible, *must* be accounted for without the postulation of certain highly specialized abilities and dispositions (to which we give the name "mind") with which we are genetically endowed and which manifest themselves, in the appropriate circumstances, at a certain stage of our development?

It is of course the traditional associations of the word "mind" that are responsible for much of the hostile reaction to Chomsky's rationalism (or "mentalism"). Many philosophers, and most notably, perhaps, Descartes, have drawn a very sharp distinction between "body" and "mind"; and they have claimed that the physiological functions and operations of the "body," unlike the workings of the "mind," are subject to the same "mechanical," or "physical," laws as the rest of the "material" world. Chomsky's position is, however, somewhat different. Like Descartes and other "mentalists," he believes that human behavior is, in part at least, undetermined by external stimuli or internal physiological states: he is thus opposed to "mechanism" (or "physicalism," in the usual sense). On the other hand, he differs from Descartes and most philosophers who would normally be called "mentalist" in that he does not subscribe to the ultimate irreducibility of the distinction between "body" and "mind." In the radio interview to which I have referred, he makes the point that "the whole issue of whether there's a physical basis for mental structures is a rather empty issue," because, in the development of modern science, "the concept 'physical' has been extended step by step to cover anything we understand," so that "when we ultimately begin to understand the properties of mind, we shall simply . . . extend the notion 'physical' to cover these properties as well." He does not even deny that it is possible in principle to account for "mental phenomena" in terms of "the physiological processes and physical processes that we now understand." It will be clear from these quotations that, although Chomsky describes himself as a "mentalist," it is mechanistic determinism, and more particularly behaviorism, to which he is opposed, and that, in contrast with such philosophers as Plato or Descartes, he might equally well be described as a "physicalist."

Conclusion

X

In the previous chapters of this book I have tried to give a clear and sympathetic account of Chomsky's views on language, and I have deliberately refrained from making any kind of critical comment that might hold up or complicate the exposition. I must not leave the reader with the impression, however, that Chomsky's position is impregnable and his critics simply misguided or malevolent. In this final chapter, therefore, I shall redress the balance somewhat by giving a more personal assessment of the significance of Chomsky's work. Although my own views are very similar to Chomsky's on most issues, there are some points on which I think he has overstated his case.

I have already said that it was Chomsky's research on the formalization of syntactic theory that constitutes his most original and probably his most enduring contribution to the scientific investigation of language; and there can be little doubt about this. He has greatly extended the scope of what is called "mathematical linguistics" and opened up a whole field of research, which is of interest not only to linguists, but also to logicians and mathematicians. Even if it were decided eventually that none of Chomsky's work on generative grammar was of any direct relevance to the description of natural languages, it would still be judged valuable by logicians and mathematicians, who are concerned with the construction and study of formal systems independently of their empirical application. I shall say no more about this point.

It is, of course, the fact that Chomsky's model of transformational grammar was designed for the analysis of natural languages and has been employed with considerable success for that purpose over the last ten or fifteen years that has attracted the attention of psychologists and philosophers. Chomsky himself has argued, as we have seen, that the findings of transformational grammar have certain very definite implications for psychology and philosophy. He has made a strong, and to my mind convincing, case against behaviorism (in its extreme form at least); and he has argued, again cogently, that the gap between human language and systems of animal communication is such that it cannot be bridged by any obvious extension of current psychological theories of "learning" based on laboratory experiments with animals. This follows from the principle of "creativity" manifest in the use of language and does not depend, it should be observed, upon the validity of any particular model of generative grammar, or indeed even upon the possibility of constructing one. I should perhaps repeat that, although Chomsky has given good reason to believe that the model of "stimulus-and-response" is incapable of accounting for *all* the facts of language behavior, he has not shown that it cannot explain *any* of them. It might well be that some of the words referring to objects in the child's environment and certain utterances that occur frequently in the repetitive situations in which he finds himself in early life are learned by him in a way that is quite reasonably described in behaviorist terms (by saying that the words and utterances are "responses" and the objects and situations are "stimuli"); and it could also be true that this part of language not only can, but must, be learned and related to the external world and the world of social activity in this way. As far as I know, there is no evidence to suggest that this view is wrong or even implausible. What Chomsky has demonstrated is that the behaviorist account of language acquisition, if it is not entirely abandoned, must be supplemented with something more substantial than rather empty appeals to "analogy."

But what of the wider philosophical issues that he has raised in his later work? Here I think that the only verdict that can be returned, on the evidence available, is that Chomsky's case for rationalism is not quite as strong as he suggests. It rests, as we have seen, upon the alleged universality of certain formal principles of sentence construction in natural languages; and he is committed to the view "that if an artificial language were constructed which violated some of these general principles, then it would not be learned at all, or at least not learned with the ease and efficiency with which a normal child will learn human language."[1] But this hypothesis, as Chomsky's critics have pointed out, is not subject to direct empirical verification. For it is obviously impracticable to bring up a child from birth with no knowledge of any natural language, exposing him only to utterances in an artificial language spoken in a full range of "normal" situations. Nor is it at all clear how one would go about designing an acceptable psychological experiment bearing less directly upon the issues involved. (Chomsky has referred to "preliminary experiments" being carried out at Harvard by George Miller: but the subjects in these experiments are apparently adults, and we cannot assume that the results would be valid for the acquisition of languages by children.)

Even if we grant for the sake of argument that the formal principles to which Chomsky appeals are universal in the sense that they do indeed hold in all languages actually spoken by human beings, are we justified in maintaining that they are peculiarly congenial to the human mind, so that any *conceivable* human language *must* conform to them? Since we cannot prove, as yet, that languages violating these principles could not be learned or used by human beings, we are entitled to withhold our assent to Chomsky's hypothesis that these formal universals are innate. An alternative explanation of their universality might be that all languages have a common origin in the remote past and have preserved the formal principles of their source.[2] Whether

[1] *The Listener*, May 30, 1968, p. 688.
[2] This point has been explicitly discussed by Chomsky in *Language and Mind* (pp. 74–75), where he argues that it "involves a serious misunderstanding of the problem at issue." It is true, as he says, that the hypothesis of common

all existing languages do in fact derive from one source is not known—and, once again, we are faced with what seems to be an unverifiable hypothesis—but it is a possibility that should be allowed for.

In so far as linguistics is an empirical science, whose purpose it is to construct a theory of the structure of human language, it is of course important that linguists should incorporate within the theory all the substantive and formal universals that can be established in the investigation of particular languages. Chomsky is right, I believe, when he says that the diversity of structures found throughout the languages of the world is less striking than the "structuralists" have claimed. On the other hand, it should be emphasized that relatively few languages have yet been described in any great depth. Syntactic research of the last few years, much of it inspired directly by Chomsky's work, seems to me to lend a fair amount of support to the adherents of "universal grammar." But the results that have been obtained so far must be regarded as very tentative; and this fact

---

origin "contributes nothing to explaining" how "the grammar of a language must be discovered by the child from the data presented to him." But this is not the problem for which the hypothesis of common origin is being proposed here as an explanation. Chomsky's assumption that certain formal principles of grammar are innate is intended to account for two problems simultaneously: (1) the universality of the principles (on the assumption that they are in fact found to be universal) and (2) the child's success in constructing the grammar of his language on the basis of the utterances he hears around him. It is the second of these questions that Chomsky regards as the more important ("the language is 'reinvented' each time it is learned, and the empirical problem to be faced by the theory of learning is how this invention of grammar can take place").

should be borne in mind when linguistic evidence is being used in philosophical arguments.

It is in any case arguable that some of the old philosophical and psychological oppositions, such as rationalism vs. empiricism, instinct vs. learning, mind vs. body, heredity vs. environment, and so on, have lost much of their force. Current work in the comparative study of animal and human behavior would suggest that behavior which is normally described as "instinctual" requires very particular environment conditions during the period of "maturation." Whether one says that such behavior is "innate" or "learned by experience" is a matter of emphasis: both "instinct" and "environment" are necessary, and neither is sufficient without the other.

As we saw at the end of the last chapter, Chomsky, though he calls himself a "mentalist," does not wish to be committed to the traditional opposition of "body" and "mind." His position would seem to be consistent with the view that the "knowledge" and "predispositions" for language, though "innate," require rather definite environmental conditions during the period of "maturation." One might go on to suggest, as an alternative to Chomsky's hypothesis, that it is not a "knowledge" of the formal principles of language as such that is innate, but a more general "faculty," which, given the right environmental conditions, will interact with these to produce linguistic competence.[3] This could still be called

---

[3] Chomsky says that he is not convinced that this is a true "alternative": he accepts that the proper environmental conditions are necessary for the maturation of innate structures (cf. *Aspects of the Theory of Syntax*, pp. 33–34). He believes that "no more is at stake than a decision as to how to apply the term 'knowledge' in a rather obscure area." He further

a "rationalist" hypothesis in the sense that it contradicts the more extreme form of empiricism. But then there are probably very few extreme empiricists. Most philosophers and psychologists would no doubt accept that some "mental faculties" are specific to human beings (although they might prefer not to use the words "mental faculty") and are both biologically and environmentally determined. Once again, it must be admitted that there is no evidence to show that this alternative hypothesis (which many scholars who call themselves "empiricists" might favor) is correct. But I am not claiming that Chomsky is wrong. What I am saying is that the evidence, so far at least, is inconclusive.

The fact that we have delivered a verdict of "not proven" on Chomsky's particularly strong form of the rationalist thesis does not mean that it is without importance. He has shown that there is nothing inherently unscientific about the assumption, or hypothesis, that competence in speaking a language implies that the speaker has in his "mind" a number of generative rules (whether they are "innate" or "learned") of a highly restricted kind and is capable of "storing" and operating upon abstract "mental structures" in the course of pro-

---

suggests that I should point out that "even the most narrow empiricist would not regard a hypothesis as devoid of empirical content because it is not directly testable in practice," that it is generally accepted by modern empiricists "that meaningful hypotheses, in general, must only meet the condition that some possible evidence have some bearing on them—that they not be entirely neutral with respect to all conceivable evidence." I did not intend to give the impression in my criticism of Chomsky's hypothesis that I regard it as meaningless or vacuous, but it may be as well to make this point explicit.

ducing or analyzing utterances. This in itself is a considerable achievement, given the strong prejudice that existed not long ago among psychologists and linguists, and perhaps also philosophers of science, against any theory that went beyond the observable data. Chomsky was surely right to challenge "the belief that the mind must be simpler in its structure than any known physical organ and that the most primitive of assumptions must be adequate to explain whatever phenomena can be observed."[4]

It would be inappropriate in a book of this nature, and impossible in the space available, to give a detailed criticism of Chomsky's theory of generative grammar from a purely linguistic point of view.[5] I must be content with two general points. The first has to do with the distinction he draws between "competence" and "performance," which was mentioned in Chapters IV and VIII. Although a distinction of this kind is undoubtedly both a theoretical and a methodological necessity in linguistics, it is by no means certain that Chomsky himself draws it in the right place. It can be argued that he describes as matters of "performance" (and, therefore, as irrelevant) a number of factors that should be handled in terms of "competence." The second point is that, on questions of detail, any linguist's judgment of what is a more "natural" or more "revealing" way of describing the data will tend to be somewhat arbitrary. Furthermore, it is not always clear when the differences between alternative descriptions of the same data are differences

[4] *Language and Mind*, p. 22.
[5] For a critical discussion of the more technical points in Chomsky's theory the reader is referred to Matthews' review of *Aspects of the Theory of Syntax*.

of substance and when they are merely differences of terminology and notation. Chomsky himself has said, of current work in generative grammar, "At present the field is in considerable ferment, and it will probably be some time before the dust begins to settle and a number of outstanding issues are even tentatively resolved."[6] He has claimed elsewhere (in more recent and more technical publications) that the differences between his own position and that of other linguists on many of these issues are purely "notational." Many will disagree with him.

I will not try to justify the two points I have just made. They have been mentioned simply to indicate that even those linguists who are generally sympathetic to Chomsky's views may differ from him on various issues. Other scholars, of course, have more fundamental objections to his theory of generative grammar.

Earlier in this chapter I said that we must at least envisage the possibility that Chomsky's theory of generative grammar will be dismissed one day, by the consensus of linguists, as irrelevant to the description of natural languages. I should add that I personally believe, and very many linguists will share this belief, that even if the attempt he has made to formalize the concepts employed in the analysis of languages should fail, the attempt itself will have immeasurably increased our understanding of these concepts and that in this respect the "Chomskyan revolution" cannot help being successful.

[6] *Language and Mind*, p. 54, fn. 6.

SHORT BIBLIOGRAPHY

INDEX

SHORT BIBLIOGRAPHY

Selected works by Chomsky

Syntactic Structures. The Hague: Mouton, 1957. This is the first of Chomsky's major publications. It is relatively non-technical and draws heavily upon his earlier, unpublished work, "The Logical Structure of Linguistic Theory."

"On Certain Formal Properties of Grammars," in *Information and Control,* II (1959), pp. 137–67. Reprinted in R. D. Luce, Bush, and Galanter, *Readings in Mathematical Psychology,* Vol. 2. New York: John Wiley, 1965.

Review of B. F. Skinner's *Verbal Behavior,* in *Language,* XXXV (1959), pp. 26–58. Reprinted in Fodor and Katz, *The Structure of Language* (which see).

"On the Notion 'Rule of Grammar,'" in *Twelfth Symposium in Applied Mathematics,* edited by Roman Jakobson. Providence, R.I.: American Mathematical Society, 1961. Quite technical.

"Formal Properties of Grammars," and (with G. A. Miller) "Introduction to the Formal Analysis of Natural Languages," in R. D. Luce, Bush and Galanter, *Handbook of Mathematical Psychology,* Vol. 2. New York: John Wiley, 1963. Also in the same volume, "Finitary Models of Language Users," by Miller and Chomsky. These three articles are very technical. They give the fullest account of Chomsky's more formal work and its possible applications than is elsewhere readily accessible.

Current Issues in Linguistic Theory. The Hague: Mouton, 1964.

Aspects of the Theory of Syntax. Cambridge, Mass.: MIT Press, 1965. This presents the first major modification of Chomsky's system of transformational grammar. It covers a wide range of topics and is quite difficult to read without a knowledge of the supporting literature.

Topics in the Theory of Generative Grammar. The Hague: Mouton, 1966. Includes a concise account of the revised version of transformational grammar and Chomsky's reply to some of his critics.

Cartesian Linguistics: A Chapter in the History of Rationalist Thought. New York: Harper & Row, 1966. Here Chomsky discusses his own views on generative grammar and the philosophy of language in relation to those of Descartes and other rationalist philosophers.

Language and Mind. New York: Harcourt, Brace & World, 1968. Based on the Beckman Lectures delivered at the University of California in 1967, it is by far the clearest statement of Chomsky's philosophy of language.

American Power and the New Mandarins. New York: Pantheon, 1969.

Other works

Bloomfield, L. *Language.* New York: Henry Holt, 1933.

Boas, F. *Handbook of American Indian Languages.* Washington, D.C.: Smithsonian Institution, 1911.

Bolinger, D. *Aspects of Language.* New York: Harcourt, Brace & World, 1968.

Dinneen, F. P. *An Introduction to General Linguistics.* New York: Holt, Rinehart and Winston, 1967. Includes excerpts from the writings of Boas, Sapir, Bloomfield, and Chomsky, with exposition.

Fodor, J. A., and Katz, J. J. *The Structure of Language: Readings in the Philosophy of Language.* Englewood Cliffs, N.J.: Prentice-Hall, 1964. Includes a number of articles by Chomsky and his associates.

Hockett, C. F. *The State of the Art.* The Hague: Mouton,

1967. A severe and forceful criticism of Chomsky's linguistic theory.

Lyons, J. *Introduction to Theoretical Linguistics*. London and New York: Cambridge University Press, 1968.

Lyons, J. (ed.). *New Horizons in Linguistics*. London: Penguin, 1970.

Marshall, J. C. Review of E. A. Esper's *Mentalism and Objectivism in Linguistics*, in *Semiotica* (in press).

Matthews, P. H. Review of Chomsky's *Aspects of the Theory of Syntax*, in *Journal of Linguistics*, III (1967), pp. 119–152.

Oldfield, R. C., and Marshall, J. C. (eds.). *Language*. London: Penguin, 1968. (Penguin Modern Psychology, UPS 10.)

Robins, R. H. *A Short History of Linguistics*. London: Longmans, 1967.

Sapir, E. *Language*. New York: Harcourt, Brace, 1921.

Addendum (1971)

Chomsky: Selected Readings. Edited by J. P. B. Allen and P. van Buren. London, New York and Toronto: Oxford University Press, 1971. An excellent selection of extracts from Chomsky's own writings arranged and linked together by the editors.

INDEX